T0160736

JUNK ENG LISH²

JUNK ENGLISH²

KEN SMITH

BLAST BOOKS NEW YORK

JUNK ENGLISH 2 © 2004 Ken Smith

Blast Books gratefully acknowledges the generous help of Don Kennison and Ken Siman.

Published by Blast Books, Inc.
P. O. Box 51, Cooper Station
New York, NY 10276-0051

ISBN 0-922233-27-6

DESIGNED BY LAURA LINDGREN

The text in this book is set in Janson.

Printed in the United States of America

First Edition 2004

10 9 8 7 6 5 4 3 2 1

For Heather

Language is the perfect instrument of empire.

—ANTONIO DE NEBRIJA,
BISHOP OF AVILA, 1492

CONTENTS

ACKNOWLEDGMENTS

This book could not have been written without the suggestions, support, and friendship of Michelle Boulé, Dorian Devins, Heather Glacken, Jamie Kelty, Don Kennison, Julie King, Doug and Susie Kirby, Jill Melamed, Litza Stark, Ken Swezey and Laura Lindgren, Dorothy Wilson, my family, and especially my parents, Herb and Anita Smith.

PREFACE TO THE NEW EDITION

Junk English, published in early September 2001, was conceived as a single book. My heart would have been lighter had it remained that way. Time and circumstance, however, dictated otherwise.

I will always remember watching the local news on September 11, hearing the stunned coanchor say repeatedly, "This is incredulous. This is absolutely incredulous!" Events that had nothing to do with language were breeding a new generation of junk English even as *Junk English* arrived in bookstores. The outflow of humbug hasn't slackened since.

Much of what was bad in our language in 2001 has grown worse. Vocabularies bulge with more words that make us less intelligent; business jargon is more prevalent; social and class jargons are more divisive; advertising cant is shriller; broadcast journalism is more illiterate; arrogance is in fashion; mendacity is an accepted professional skill; felicity is vanishing.

Language as a tool of obfuscation has plumbed new depths. Political chicanery, relying on legal definitions of plain words such as *is* or *torture*, has reached new heights.

A casual disregard for clarity and precision in language has served us poorly since September 2001. Sloppy language has resulted in poor rationale and flawed thinking, priming us for misunderstanding and allowing guile and gibberish to go unrecognized and unchallenged.

While these developments are troubling, there is also reason for hope. The increased attention given to the subject of junk English since the publication of *Junk English*—an accident of timing, not an instance of cause and effect—is cheering. *Junk English* was received with enthusiasm, and many readers generously offered insights and suggestions, for which I am grateful. I have incorporated a number of them into this book.

I hope that this new compendium will prove useful. I also hope that these books together will help us to recognize when our language is serving us honestly and when it is junk.

July 2004

A MESSAGE FROM KEN

Junk English takes many forms. It is the salesperson who describes a product as *high quality* and a *real value*, the coworker who writes of the *positive side of the consumer equation*, the politician who speaks of *sensible reform*, the television analyst who talks of *anomalous paradigms*, your best friend who says *Let's do lunch!*

All of us use junk English, often many times a day. That does not make it more forgivable, but more troubling.

Junk English is much more than sloppy grammar. It is a hash of human frailties and cultural license: spurning the language of the educated yet spawning its own pretentious words and phrases, favoring appearance over substance, broadness over precision, and loudness above all. It is sometimes innocent, sometimes lazy, sometimes well intended, but most often it is a trick we play on ourselves to make the unremarkable seem important. Its scope has been widened by politicians, business executives, and the PR and advertising industries in their employ, who use it to spread fog before facts they would rather keep hidden. The result is Edmund Burke's tyranny of the multitude merged with George Orwell's Newspeak, a world of humbug in which the more we read and hear, the less we know.

Junk English is the linguistic equivalent of junk food—ingest it long enough and your brain goes soft.

This book is a catalog of observations, not a text of grammar or style. I have salted it liberally with examples from everyday life. The errors and abuses are blatant and familiar; you will not need a degree in English to recognize them.

This book is also an overview of an encyclopedic subject. Much had to be pared away, particularly if it fell within wide-ranging topics. If your favorite atrocity is missing, I hope that you will understand. My intent was to keep this book small and handy so that it would be useful to a spectrum of people, for junk English will not go away until all of us recognize it.

This book is judgmental. Some may be uncomfortable with that. But we have been nonjudgmental for so long that abominations like *confab* and *smartize* and *impactful* and *conversating* have multiplied in our language and will continue to do so until we raise our hands in unison and say, "Pardon me, but what the hell does that mean?"

Junk English is not inevitable. We made it. We can make it go away. Thus this book.

July 2001

All of the examples in this book (quoted without correction of typographical or grammatical error) were taken from life: newspaper and magazine articles; radio and television commentators; advertisements and editorials. None came from internal business or political memoranda; all were intended to be understood by ordinary people.

Actionable. This legal term has become popular with military spokespeople who use it as an empty adjective.

> Mr. Rumsfeld said that the Iraqis had learned how to conceal the precise actionable location of military targets.

Actionable is also used as a GROOVY LINGO substitute for *usable.*

> We believe that for employee research to be truly valuable, results must be actionable.

Actionable intelligence has become the stylish way to say *useful information.*

Understand the key forces influencing your market, gather focused actionable intelligence, and make informed business decisions. Only then you can truly compete and win.

Adjust generally means to make a minor CHANGE. When, instead, a change is great, greater words are needed: *recast, overhaul,* even simply *change.* To use *adjust* where a sweeping change has occurred is dishonest.

> We have adjusted our policy toward investment in mainland China to allow companies to include it in their global strategy.

> Groups have petitioned newspapers in the past to close what has been termed the "newspaper loophole" that allows a person to purchase handguns through classified ads without federal background checks. We have adjusted our policy to address this concern.

Asymmetric warfare, sometimes lengthened to *asymmetrical warfare,* replaces what used to be called *guerrilla warfare,* perhaps to give the impression that something old is something new. It describes the tactics used by weak forces to battle strong forces—ambushes, hidden bombs, etc.—which are as old as recorded history, including that of the United States, whose colonists used them to fight the British and gain independence.

Because asymmetric warfare is used by the weak, and because the weak usually lose, and because history is written by the winners, it is also referred to as *dirty fighting.*

Atrocities. Think of an absurd nonword such as *unfactual.* Type it into a Web search engine and you'll find several examples of it in use.

> A serious scholar will use internet materials with great caution, given the abundance of unfactual and inaccurate material.

The freedom to invent new words is a hallmark of a living language. Words that are coined out of ignorance, laziness, or an impulse to sound impressive, however, are atrocities.

Atrocities are disquieting. Although they are jarring to some, they are obviously not so to those who use them.

accidented = injured, killed
agreeance = agreement
clueful = smart, wise
consense = agree
conversate = converse
counterintuiting = contradicting
delegitimate = belittle
disenable = disable
dissatisfication = dissatisfaction
efforting = attempting
exceedance = excess, overrun
exfiltrated = ran away
genericized = generic
idiocity = idiocy
impactful = effective
incent = encourage

interpretate = interpret
mentee = trainee, novice, apprentice
mindshare, brainshare = attention
mindspace = mind
officing = working
orientate = orient
planful = well planned, prepared
proact = anticipate
subliminable = subliminal
timezone = time
trialling = testing
visioning = thinking, creating
wordify = write

Average. When applied to concepts such as net worth and income this word is often misused by politicians as a substitute for *median* and *mean*, which can be two widely different numbers. *Average* becomes a tool in the old trick of lying with statistics. For example, three families with annual incomes of $25,000, $45,000, and $500,000 would have a median income of $45,000 but a mean income of $190,000. Politicians who want to pass a tax cut sell it on the premise that it will refund X dollars to the "average" family, yet they may be referring to a very exclusive average—in this example, the $190,000 mean. Without knowing the median and the mean, the average could be either.

Bad guys, good guys. The use of this paired term conveys a firm, or possibly simpleminded, view of human behavior. It has become popular to see the world through a narrow lens that allows for only bad guys and good guys, and the allure is understandable. It eliminates doubt, questions, and time-wasting reflection. It is balm to a practical people stuck on a complicated planet.

Marine Fighter Training Squadron-401 stays busy by acting like bad guys, so other squadrons can prepare themselves by practicing being the good guys.

I think we need Christian heroes who are willing to sacrifice their way of life for a long time. We need men who are clad in the armour of God to give up years of their lives and fellowship with their churches. Men who know every mind game Islam can play on them going in. That way we can get the bad guys and leave the good guys alone. To me, that would be the Christian way to handle the problem.

Rumsfeld said the situation in Afghanistan is very confused. "It is not a neat situation where all the good guys are here and the bad guys are there," he said.

Bargain means worth more than its cost. A thing can be expensive and still be thought of as a bargain—as in *Clearly, even with anticipated cost increases, clean water remains a bargain*—yet the word is often misused by salespeople as a synonym for *inexpensive*. Something can be inexpensive and not be a bargain.

CRUISING THE ERIE CANAL IS A REAL BARGAIN

They buy their food at the local store, where the shelves are stocked with expired junk food at bargain prices.

We are proud to offer this Central North Dakota land for sale.... A real bargain!

Basis appears most frequently as an anchor for long-winded idiomatic expressions. *What is the basis for this?* can be expressed as *Why?* with no loss of meaning.

on a case-by-case basis = one by one
on a consistent basis = regularly
on a continuous basis = continuously
on a daily basis = daily
on a day-in day-out basis = daily
on a global basis = internationally
on a going-forward basis = in the future
on a minute-by-minute basis = continually
on a moment-by-moment basis = continually
on a regular basis = regularly
on a rush basis = quickly
on an accelerated basis = quickly

on an interim basis = temporarily
on an ongoing basis = continually

Benefit. To benefit is to be helped by or to profit from something. It is easy, however, to slip into using *benefit* as an affected substitute for *help* or *improve*.

What Author Benefited You the Most Spiritually?

When you drink organic coffee you benefit yourself, the farmer, and the environment.

"I knew I wasn't going to benefit myself if I didn't take the first step," she said. "I was determined to benefit myself." And benefit she did.

Build, meaning to grow or to generate, is frequently employed as a substitute for *improve* and *strengthen.* Because building something is seen as good, the word has become common in business language in phrases such as *build the client base* [get customers], *build market share* [steal customers from competitors], *build on current momentum* [exploit the moment], *build wealth* [get money], *build positive sales momentum* [get more money], and *build a relationship with* [get more information about].

Build is sometimes used as a noun to mean increase or surge.

A current focus area is managing the Holiday Inventory build.

Capital intensive. In the world of commerce *capital intensive* describes a business whose expenses are more in equipment than in labor. It is also now used as PRETENTIOUS LANGUAGE for *costly* or *expensive*.

> In order to make it less capital intensive to our customers and potential customers, we are selling 2 port desktops at $200 and 4 port desktops at $400.

Change is generally looked upon favorably in America, although at times change is inconvenient or obviously not to our advantage or it calls to attention existing flaws. On these occasions those who must mention a change do not want to call it that. The word is softened to ADJUST, or to *re-* verbs such as *readjust* and *realign*.

> We have to realign our priorities.

> After March 15 rates can adjust every six months.

Change is also avoided by those who want a word that sounds more impressive. POWERPOINT PEOPLE use *reformat*, GROOVY LINGO faddists use *morph*, others use *transform*. *Sweeping change*, a HACK-NEYED EXPRESSION, has been replaced by other hackneyed expressions such as *sea change*, *paradigm shift*, or the very impressive *paradigmatic shift*.

> If we don't reformat the way we run our charity work, it may lead to a horrible disaster.

> Can executive management morph their companies?

> There's a real sea change in the way doctors are facing the world, and in the way patients are facing the world.

> Cyber short stories is just part of the new paradigm shift in the teaching of English.

The optimism with which we view change is evident in *change agent*, a label affixed to a person in an organization who shakes things up. As this often involves firing people, the label also gives a vaguely approving cast to what used to be called a *hatchet man*.

Classroom Cacophony. American schools—as well as American museums, hospitals, libraries, and other institutions—have in recent years embraced the business tenets of efficiency, productivity, and competition. This has brought with it a language and vocabulary more suited to sales consultants and MBAs than to Mr. Peepers and Miss Louise. Add to this the cowardly mush of lawsuit avoidance and political correctness, and the halls of learning have become towers of babel.

academic therapist = tutor

achievement time, advisory time, time to care = homeroom

activity co-requisite required = laboratory required

alternative instruction room, reinforcement room, reflection room =
    detention

brief constructed response = paragraph

capstone experience = final exam

deliver educational services = teach

educational facilitator = teacher, librarian, guidance counselor

extended constructed response = essay

Family and Consumer Science = Home Economics [formerly
    Domestic Science]

formative assessment = test

front-line educator = teacher

learners = students

learning cottage = classroom trailer

learning environment = classroom, school

learning program = course

modeling strategies = learning

selected response = multiple choice

Service Learning = shop class

standard units of credit = classes

sustained silent reading (SSR) = reading

text-to-text connections = comparing books

The coalition, the coalition of the willing. The word *coalition*
is a synonym for *alliance* and *bloc* and was used by the United
States to describe the nations that invaded Iraq in 1991. The rou-
tine practice of U.S. politicians and mass media of referring to the

people that invaded and occupied Iraq in 2003 solely as *the coalition* or as *coalition forces* or *coalition troops* is misleading because the occupation was an overwhelmingly American effort. The casual mixing of *coalition* with references to the United States, sometimes in the same sentence, betrays the absurdity of the phrase.

> Some 25 people were killed and some 130 wounded in a suicide blast outside coalition headquarters in Baghdad in the boldest assault yet on the symbol of U.S. power in Iraq.

> When the coalition forces entered Iraq to liberate its people, Arabs and Muslims started screaming for Iraq to be freed from the occupation of the United States, as if Iraqis were free under Saddam.

This so-called coalition was initially labeled *the coalition of the willing* to suggest that it was a group bound together by enthusiasm. But there wasn't much of a group to bind, and the cumbersome suffix fell when Baghdad did.

In 2004 *the coalition* was replaced by *the multinational force*—more militaristic and just as misleading.

Comfort Words. Nebulous nouns—FACTOR, *function, status, system,* and their kind—when used to modify already abstract nouns that need no modification, are like hot fudge poured over fudge-flavored ice cream.

business entity = business
celebrity status, health status = celebrity, health
cost factor = cost

crisis situation = crisis
disaster scenario = disaster
display environment = display
food item = food
funding purposes = funding
job function = job
landfall location = landfall
large or *small format* = large, small
opportunity space = opportunity
planning phase = planning
price, talent, tension, or *interest level* = price, talent, tension, interest
road surface = road
storm event = storm
tonsillectomy procedure, abortion procedure = tonsillectomy, abortion
training opportunities = training
weapon system = weapon [or better: gun, bomb, plane, etc.]
weather conditions = weather

Computer Language. Various words among the various jargons associated with computers have infiltrated everyday English—not just office language but language used at home as well. While this is understandable, given the prevalence of computers in our lives, we should be aware of the extent of this jargon's infestation, and be mindful when we find ourselves talking, or being talked to, as if we were machines.

activate = turn on
capture = record
configuration = setup

de-install, *delete* = remove
deselect = reject
execute = start, begin, enact, use
feedback, *input* = opinion, suggestions, insight
inputs = parts
interactive = engaging
opt in = accept
opt out = refuse
output = result, work
plugged in = aware
reformat = change, alter, rework, revise
unsubscribe = cancel
wired = built
zeroize = reset

Conspiracy theory. Conspiracies do take place and theories about them can be well reasoned and supported by substantive evidence. *Conspiracy theory*, however, has become a pejorative term applied to valid theories as readily as to those that involve lizard people or UFOs. As a term of condemnation *conspiracy theory* is now being applied broadly to discredit opinions or ideas—and those who have them—that may not involve conspiracies at all, or whose suspected conspiracies, while unsettling to contemplate, may not be far-fetched or implausible. The latitude of what one considers conspiracy theory is proportioned to the range of what one considers acceptable thought.

The idea that the possible war against Iraq is to do with oil really makes no sense. Why would you spend billions of pounds attacking Iraq, when Saddam has a track record of being very happy to overproduce and provide the West with cheap oil? Blair is correct to call it an oil conspiracy theory.

Conspiracy fans can have a field day if Sen. John Kerry wins the Democratic nomination for president, as it appears at this time he will. Conspiracy buffs can say that, once more, the Establishment has won.

Speaking before the UN General Assembly, the president said, "We must speak the truth about terror. Let us never tolerate outrageous conspiracy theories concerning the attacks of September the eleventh, malicious lies that attempt to shift the blame away from the terrorists themselves, away from the guilty."

Consumer has ousted *shopper, purchaser,* and *customer* in the lexicon of commerce, and it is replacing dozens of other specific human designations as well, such as *patient* and *listener.*

"Consumer participation" is simply when consumers formally give input into any part of the policies or planning of a mental health service.

More music is being consumed than at any time in history, it's just that less of it is being paid for.

Consumers is passive and powerless compared to *citizens* and mindless compared to *people,* yet it has replaced these words as well.

Consumers will only obtain true options in housing and transportation if they offset the political influence of the sprawl lobby.

Consumers should not be an afterthought in setting agricultural policy.

The phrase *consumer-driven* is a EUPHEMISM that indicates that whatever follows it—as in *consumer-driven health care*—is something that you will have to pay for.

Content provider lumps together people—animators, salespeople, writers, etc.—with companies, making it unclear if what is being referred to is a human being or a corporation.

A content provider may request your Personal Information directly or you may provide it to them as part of the registration process.

The Internet Streaming Media Alliance announced that it is assembling a panel of outside experts to advise the alliance on issues critical to the content provider community.

NEITHER WE NOR ANY CONTENT PROVIDER MAKES ANY WARRANTY ABOUT THE ACCURACY, RELIABILITY, COMPLETENESS, TIMELINESS, SUFFICIENCY, OR QUALITY OF THE SITE.

Cool is the saddest word in junk English. It is the trumpet that heralds a society mired in a perpetual superficial adolescence.

Check out the latest cool pencil from Cool Valley Pencils. This Alien pencil comes with a glow in the dark Alien head topper.

Cool does not deserve such a fate. As an exclamation of delight, it expresses genuine enthusiasm. But more often than not, the use of *cool* by an adult as an all-purpose adjective gives an impression of immaturity and makes the user sound dumb.

It's a totally cool shrub, but it's my understanding you need one male and at least two females to get the berries.

They brought Chinese spaghetti for dinner, and along with it they had brought a really cool vegetable that they'd grown in their own garden.

I'm a bit worried about the pipes but I'm looking forward to buying all those cool plumbing tools, like pipe benders and cutters and stuff.

This example shows how cool a simple help from a company can result in a very cool tax reduction.

Come on in for the coolest RETIREMENT PLANNING around!

Core competencies is the current flashy way to say *what we do best.* To be competent, however, is merely to be capable, not outstanding. *Core competencies* therefore implies only what we do passably well, which is nothing to brag about.

That is the SafeNet difference. Our core competencies set us miles apart from our competitor.

From Georgia Tech research labs to Savannah's ports complex and beyond, our technology base is creating world-class core competencies.

Credible. To be credible is to be trustworthy, but the word often appears in contexts where all that is intended is to be persuasive— to have the mere appearance of credibility, which is not credible.

You need a credible message, credible messengers inside and outside your organization, and effective channels for communication.

Crybaby Verbs. Many nouns also have a verb form. Some of the newest noun-verbs, however, are affected. They irritate and they draw attention to themselves rather than to the idea being expressed. People may have grumbled when *pirate* was first used for *steal* or *market* for *sell*, noun-verbs that eventually matured into anonymity. Perhaps these brats will do likewise. It would be better, however, if they stayed nouns.

architect = design, build, form
benchmark = gauge
broker = make, arrange
cave = surrender
conference = discuss, talk
effort = attempt

fast track = speed, hasten
guilt = shame
leverage = use
mainstream = make common
office = run an office
solution = solve
spike = cancel
transition = change, move
whiteboard = describe, explain
wordsmith = write

Customer relationship management, often abbreviated to the INITIALISM *CRM*, is also sometimes called *relationship marketing*, *real-time marketing*, and *customer intimacy* and is what happens when companies try to sell their ability to anticipate customer needs and thus increase sales. Any such ability exists, however, because CRM divisions collect, record, organize, retrieve, and disseminate vast quantities of information about you. The data collection is sometimes voluntary, but it is also accomplished through *data partnering* [buying information about you from other companies], *data mining* [the computer equivalent of "dumpster diving"], *behavioral mapping* [spying], and *retail ethnography* [spying on you while you shop]. The promoters of customer relationship management want you to think of CRM as a EUPHEMISM for its outcome—personal service—rather than for its hidden workings—invasion of your privacy.

Deliverables. Businesspeople are practical and want those who work for them to produce things that have a physical existence, such as a product, model, or prototype, or a report, memo, chart, list, diagram, or budget plan. But these have been replaced by a blanket term, *deliverables*.

> E-commerce can also involve online deliverables [products], such as software or music that can be downloaded.

> It's particularly useful for sending small deliverables [files] such as a password, a photograph, or the simple solution to a problem.

Deliverables, contrary to its original purpose, is now substituted for intangible ideas such as *advice, goals, ideas, understanding, confidence, perspective, energy, validation, structure*, and *caring*.

> Today's economies are "service oriented," and the exact type of "service" we are talking about is that of "non-physical" deliverables like information, analysis, processing, storage, security, identity, and so on.

Deregulate and **deregulation** sound like progressive measures, but *to deregulate* can mean freeing or plundering; *deregulation* can mean emancipation or legal robbery—or anything in between. The endless arguments over deregulation are therefore pointless: what's at issue is the intent behind it.

> Government should deregulate [unfetter] the utilities, and let the competitive market process do the regulating [governing], the cost-cutting, the improving of quality, and the innovating that characterize economic free choice wherever it exists.

> Deregulation [unchecked capitalism] and corporate greed are commonly cited as the cause of the soaring prices, rolling blackouts, and utility bankruptcies that now plague the state.

Detainee. A person who has been involuntarily locked in a room or a cage is commonly thought of as a prisoner, while *detainment* implies a short, temporary interruption. The mass media, however, have embraced governmental language, and now prisoners have become *detainees*, thus destroying a critical distinction along with the concept of innocent until proven guilty. Casually mixing *detainee* with references to prisoners and imprisonment is lunacy, but it has become common.

> After two and a half months there still is no accusation. That means, the detainees still don't know for what reason they are imprisoned.

> The detainees were released in a complex prisoner swap between Israel and the Lebanese militant group, Hezbollah.

Disease. We no longer have *disease*, or *illness*, or *sickness*. Instead we are beset by *challenges, conditions, disabilities, disorders, dysfunctions, impairments*, and *syndromes*. This comes partly from an odd desire to classify more of us as sick and partly from a desire not to affix labels that seem blunt or unkind—*visually impaired*, for example, sounds gentler than *blind*. It has led, in at least one instance, to four generations of EUPHEMISM: *crippled* became *handicapped*, then *disabled*, then *differently abled*, then *other-abled*. Others currently in vogue include:

congenital disability = birth defect
emotionally disordered = neurotic, crazy
exceptional, special = retarded
mentally disabled = insane, feebleminded
physically challenged, mobility impaired = crippled, lame

Drug companies have taken advantage of this trend by transforming conditions that may fall within the range of normal but are socially unacceptable, or that may be abnormal but are effectively treatable through drugless therapy, into physical illnesses whose symptoms can be altered with pills.

Amotivational Syndrome = apathy, dullness, indolence, laziness
Attention Deficit Hyperactivity Disorder = fidgeting, inattention
Erectile Dysfunction = impotence
Generalized Anxiety Disorder = worry, nervousness
Major Depressive Disorder = dejection, melancholy
Oppositional Defiance Disorder = rebelliousness, questioning
    authority
Social Anxiety Disorder = shyness

Downsize is an ugly way to say *reduce* or *reduction,* as in *Russia's military downsizing is good for all.* It also frequently appears as an adjective.

> The networks are moving toward a "hybrid" model involving a downsized fall season with fewer new shows.

> Can't we just say "No!" to buying the downsized potato chip bag or the more expensive postage stamps or the jacked-up electricity?

Downsize's most infamous application is as a EUPHEMISM for *laying off*—formerly known as *firing*—people. It performs the impressive feat of removing humans from a description of something that happens exclusively to humans. *Downsizing* merely states that an organization has become smaller without saying how.

> The company has been downsizing over the last three months in response to the current economic downturn.

> The fact that corporate downsizing is good for the economy is indisputable, Adams said, adding that anybody with an I.Q. of more than 80 would agree.

The word *downsized* has become so familiar that even some of those who have been fired now call themselves *downsized,* passively accepting this bland term or perhaps grateful to have a word to distinguish themselves from people who are fired for incompetency.

> I was downsized out of a 12-year job that I hoped would give me five more years so I could retire and draw social security.

I currently have a lot of time on my hands for knitting as I was downsized at my job as a children's crisis mental health clinician.

Due diligence, like PREEMPTION, is a legal term that has been dragged into everyday vocabulary. It is an unnecessarily exotic alternate to ordinary English words such as *thoroughness, homework*, and just plain *diligence*.

Due diligence demands that they use contraceptives in all sexual acts that are not expressly intended to result in pregnancy.

It seems that in an effort to prove his point, the author did not always use due-diligence to verify all the information, and as such weakens his case.

Is there anything cuter than a puppy? Unfortunately, puppies grow up and unless you have done due diligence, you may be in for some surprises.

Earn money. To *earn money* means to receive it in return for work. One cannot *earn* money effortlessly; that is to *get* money.

> Free and Easy way to make lots of money. Earn Money While You Sleep!!!!

Educate, once associated with lofty notions of knowledge and worldliness, has become a mask for terms describing less venerable activities such as *train, indoctrinate, manipulate, sell, brainwash,* and other activities that generally involve profiting at someone else's expense.

> Our educated sales associates will be on hand to assist you.

> If planners are not getting new clients, it's a wake-up call that we still have a lot more work to do educating consumers about the value of planners in their lives.

> Call today to educate yourself with the fascinating opportunities in the world of real estate.

Rob Sisco, president of Nielsen Music, said lawsuits by the RIAA have rekindled sales, not by striking fear in music pirates but by educating users.

Empower. Respect, freedom, self-confidence, and similar states have all been overtaken by one—empowerment. To many, power is all that matters nowadays.

Kandi Grossman loves being a woman and feels empowered when she belly dances.

Forgiveness is Self-Empowerment

Empower Your Subscribers with MyCaller. No more boring ringback tones.

Empower your life with the largest collection of happiness quotes on the web.

Declarations such as "Empower Customers to Solve Problems" merely describe a shifting of responsibility and workload. People thus "empowered" end up frustrated, overworked, and angry, not more powerful.

See also GROOVY LINGO and LEFTIST LANGUAGE.

Euphemism as Art. The early twenty-first century may someday be recognized as the golden age of the euphemism. It is America's most underappreciated creative form of expression. Renaming biblical creationism *Intelligent Design*, for example, was not only a work of shrewd calculation, it was a work of art.

action figure = boy's doll
biblical preservationist = Christian fundamentalist
biosolids = sewage sludge
decrease in habitat = increase in people (less room for wildlife)
detection technology = spyware
document management = shredding
electronic pasteurization = radiation
e-sports = video gaming
faith-based = religious
family values = conservative Christian values
forward-looking statements = guesses
functional food = genetically altered food
highly leveraged = deep in debt
inappropriate gift = bribe
investigational medication = experimental drug
moral clarity, moral certitude = arrogance, smugness
nutrient enhanced = chemical injected, drug injected
perception management, public diplomacy = propaganda
pro-growth tax policies = tax cuts for the rich
ready meals = tv dinners
service-level adjustments = budget cuts
sex worker = prostitute
superpremium ice cream = high-fat ice cream
video news release = propaganda disguised as news

Factor. Just when it seemed that the overuse, misuse, and abuse of this word could get no worse, it did. *Factor* is routinely tacked onto casual and nonsense words—*wow factor, whoa factor, booty factor, ah-ha factor, hassle factor, wimp factor*—and hundreds of others, less obvious, as well.

A couple of hours in the evening using visual aids and handouts can enlighten any homeowner and remove the fear and ignorance factor.

So how do you choose between these institutions if not by quality of education? Well, there's the prestige factor of course.

The reliability factor: Selecting a real estate agent who can best represent your interests.

Where the kitchen is going to be continually used, you really wonder whether the utensils are going to have time to be cleaned, and you've got the toilet factor, and in some of these communities there are problems with the housing.

Factor is routinely substituted for *variable*. It is also substituted for words such as *cause* and *role*, and inflated by adjectives into *key factor* and *major factor.* Calling something a *risk factor,* or a *major risk factor,* is only to say that it is a cause.

> Since many overweight people suffer from undiagnosed diabetes—itself a major risk factor for kidney disease—the risk of possible kidney damage is real.

> Find out what your Osteoporosis Risk factor is by taking a FREE simple interactive test.

> Obesity Now Recognized as a Major Risk Factor for Heart Disease.

Factual is a useful adjective when modifying nouns that can be either factual or fictional (a factual drama). Sometimes, however, *factual* appears where it is either unnecessary or overkill.

> Factual databases in biomedicine constitute a rich source of information for practitioners and lay users.

> Now, he won't let me into his apartment, and he won't let me see inside the bag, so I'm just drawing a conclusion and stating it as a factual truth.

> I would tend to steer away from those factual fact-based activities and try to lead students into the higher-level thinking.

Free speech zone. In the 1990s several American universities established free speech zones, ostensibly to allow students to express their opinions vocally without disturbing classes, but really to accommodate two academic political dogmas that are at odds with each other: free speech and political correctness. Students were allowed to voice their opinions without offending anyone because they were in places where no one would hear them. The idea has now been adopted by American cities and by the federal government. A free speech zone—also sometimes called a demonstration zone—is a small area, usually surrounded by barricades and police. It is often in a remote place, following the university model, as its purpose is to allow people to speak where they will not be heard.

Friendly. *Animal friendly. Ozone friendly. Dolphin friendly. Environmentally friendly.* Being a friend to a species or a gas means— what? Companies that advertise their products as *friendly* leave it to the customers' imagination. That's not very friendly.

Globalization is a EUPHEMISM for *world capitalism* and *corporate internationalism*.

Globalization has led to increased poverty, injustice, subordination, anti-solidarity, and ecological disasters.

Globalization has brought little but good news to those with the products, skills, and resources to market worldwide.

Monsanto is a lead player in the globalization of agriculture.

Recent studies show that the top priority for 80% of American CEOs is globalization.

Going forward has become popular in the business world and has spilled into everyday language—as an awkward substitute for *from now on*.

All of our expenses ought to be covered going forward.

Please use these for your editor's drafts going forward, or let me know if this causes any difficulty.

Bioinformatics is a universal tool. Virtually, all progress going forward is going to benefit from that tool.

Going forward is evidently not enough for some, who instead use *on a going-forward basis* and *on a go forward basis.*

Our job on a go forward basis is to realize the potential of our people, our company, and increase the stock price.

The past risk posed by gasoline components to groundwater is simply not relevant in assessing the same risk on a going-forward basis.

See also BASIS.

Granular is used as a forced metaphor for *precise, detailed,* or *increment.*

Each separate component of a system can have a different granular level of security.

Strangely enough, many marketers are not taking full advantage of the highly granulated tracking tools currently available to enhance campaign success.

Possible granularities are: YEAR; MONTH; DAY; HOUR; MINUTE; SECOND; FRACTION. The lowest level of granularity is YEAR to YEAR.

Groovy Lingo is the lexical equivalent of a middle-aged man in a business suit wearing his hair in a ponytail.

best practices, best processes = industry standard
brand = logo, name, person, product
coalescence = gathering, merging
competencies = skills
conceptualize = envision, imagine
core = central, essential, fundamental
edgy = provocative, bold, daring, brazen
emerging = new
empower = help, ease, assist, aid
endgame = conclusion
exit strategy = outcome, goal, way out
future-proof = stable, lasting, durable
gatekeeper = authority, guard, block
holistic = broad
immersive = engaging, fascinating
impact = affect, effect
implement = begin, enact
leverage = control, power
luminous = brilliant, accomplished, good
magnet = attractor
mandate = goal, require, order, decree
matrix = network, chart, outline
mentoring = guidance
metrics = standard, guide
migrate = move, switch
morph = turn, change
negative = bad, no

on demand = at any time

on message, on task, on topic = undeviating

pilot = administer, guide

positive = good, yes

privatize = give away, hand over, sell off

proactive = active, aggressive, belligerent, bold, foresighted

pushback = criticism

resonance = meaning

robust = strong

scaleable = adaptable

seamless = easy, effortless

stealth = secret, quiet

strategy = plan

synergy = cooperation

transparency = openness, honesty

vehicle = method

virtual = imitation

Hackneyed expressions are colorful phrases that may delight at first, but as they are widely adopted they become trite and trap us in narrow mental ruts, reducing our ability to formulate original expression.

a level playing field = fairness
a no-brainer = obvious
a reality check = perspective, reassurance
a slam dunk = guaranteed
across the board = everywhere
ahead of the curve = progressive
at the end of the day = finally, eventually
ballpark figure = estimate
brainstorming session = a meeting
cover all the bases = be thorough
game plan = plan, approach
give me a heads up = let me know
heavy lifting = hard work
in the loop = aware
it's not rocket science = it's easy
on the fast track = moving

on the same page = in agreement
outside the box = differently, creatively
paradigm shift = change
proven track record = record
pushing the envelope = daring, bold
put it to bed = complete it, end it
take it to the next level = improve, advance
the big picture = an overview
the inside track = an advantage
up to my eyeballs = overwhelmed
wake-up call = warning

Hate speech, hate crime. It is understandable that a society would want to make clear its rejection of bias. That, however, is best accomplished through the unbiased enforcement of unbiased laws, not by employing an alarmist term that breeds divisiveness and an Orwellian term that makes a crime of an emotion.

The injustices covered by the term *hate crime*—prejudice, trespass, assault—are serious offenses, described by words that already exist. To prosecute something as a *hate crime* is to say that, for example, white-on-white assault spurred by lust or revenge is not as criminal as white-on-black assault spurred by hate.

Hate crime and *hate speech* are subjective labels prone to misapplication and abuse. That is worrisome, given that they can be used to throw people into jail. They are sometimes affixed to crimes that are not motivated by hate, or to speech that does not inspire hate in others. Words and jokes, for example, may be disrespectful or even demeaning, or may promote misunderstanding or mockery, which is wrong—but it is not the same as hate, and to claim that those who say such things have perpetrated a hate crime is to overstate the point. Worse, some affix these labels to legitimate expressions of reasoned opinion or civic criticism in an attempt to censor what is permissible in public discourse.

> The Democratic field has engaged in political hate speech for the past six months.

> A University of British Columbia women's studies professor who criticized U.S. foreign policy has been accused of a hate crime—publicly inciting hatred against Americans.

Hero is a subjective word often misapplied to people who have done nothing heroic. However much we may wish to comfort grieving relatives, innocent people who perish in TERRORIST attacks are not *heroes* unless they performed some heroic act. Dying unexpectedly makes one a *victim* or a *casualty* but not a *hero*, no matter how horrendous the cause of death.

> A presidential proclamation has been delivered to commemorate Patriot Day, a day to recognize the events of September 11 and the heroes who perished in the terrorist attacks.

Highly is a common parasitic modifier and serves as an unnecessary crutch to formerly independent words such as *detailed, flammable, improbable, lucrative, nutritious, original, secret,* and *toxic.* Like TOTALLY and *virtually,* this word is also often meant to intensify—a GROOVY LINGO substitute for *very.*

highly accountable = responsible
highly adept = masterful
highly articulate = eloquent
highly committed = dedicated
highly compelling = moving
highly competent = talented
highly doubtful = unlikely
highly encourage = urge
highly entertaining = terrific
highly experienced = accomplished
highly functional = helpful
highly informative = enlightening
highly intelligent = brilliant
highly motivated = ambitious
highly overrated = unsatisfying
highly placed = important
highly pleased = delighted
highly political = contentious
highly productive = profitable
highly professional = respectable
highly profitable = lucrative
highly publicized = ballyhooed
highly recommended = acclaimed
highly successful = prosperous
highly trained = skilled
highly unlikely = improbable

Holistic and **holistically,** sometimes used as GROOVY LINGO and
LEFTIST LANGUAGE substitutes for *broad, inclusive, comprehensive,*

and *whole*, often have no meaning at all. They are embraced by groups as disparate as businesspeople, evangelicals, new agers, and academics, whose members all use *holistic* and *holistically* when they want to impress.

Home on the Range, a sprawling ranch where holistically managed grass-fed beef cattle are raised.

The integration and intervention of holistic Christian health care practices strive for unique outcomes within a multifaith context.

ALOE VERA: HOLISTICALLY PERFECT PLANT

While this solution may be logically correct, we know that it is not Holistically logical.

Read about how Ford manages its supply chain holistically.

Nature's Finest products are all-natural, super premium pet foods formulated with the holistically-oriented pet owner in mind.

INTRODUCING HSG's HOLISTIC PEST MANAGEMENT (HPM) SYSTEMS TECHNOLOGIES ONLINE ADVISORY CONSULTATION SUCCESS ROACH SYSTEM FOR REPELLING, TRAPPING, AND ELIMINATING ALL COCKROACHES.

Homeland. Hitler's Germany was known as the Fatherland, Stalin's Russia the Motherland. American politicians have followed their examples by replacing the words *country* and *nation* with *homeland*, evidently in the hope that it will make us more patriotic. The media have obediently complied. *Homeland* appears most frequently in the phrase *homeland security*, a more emotive term than *national defense*.

The United States Tuesday ratcheted up security on land, at sea and in the air following an "orange alert" that terrorists may again be planning to attack the homeland—possibly using weapons of mass destruction, senior officials fear.

The FBI is warning law enforcement in a new security advisory to be alert for signs of a biological or chemical attack against the homeland by al-Qaida terrorists over the next few weeks.

In the process of is a phrase that can be excised wherever it is found, sometimes leaving the *in,* with no loss of meaning.

Our firm takes an active part in [the process of] setting professional standards in accounting and auditing.

The accident is [in the process of] being cleared from the roadway.

While [in the process of] placing your order, you might ask: Do you guarantee safe shopping?

Inappropriate. What exactly is encompassed by *inappropriate* is often a mystery. It can stand for anything from impoliteness to criminal activity.

Any apparent inappropriate use of the Purchasing Authority will be discussed with the ordering department.

The physician's inappropriate behavior left the runner with no alternative but to sue.

Since your daughter has already befriended someone with inappropriate values, let her know that you disapprove.

A fast and thorough response to inappropriate cat urination will most always resolve the problem.

Infomercial. Whether a commercial lasts thirty seconds or thirty minutes, it is still a commercial.

See also MONGRELS.

Initialisms. Take an idea that is clear in one simple word, give it instead a long-winded name, then compress the name into an initialism. Now you've got an idea that's as clear as mud. The most direct way to say, for example, *return on investment* is to use the word *profit*, not the initialism *ROI*, which merely adds another layer of obfuscation.

Initialisms create two-steps-removed terms such as *ED* for impotence, *MLM* for pyramid scams, and *HNWI* for rich people.

BLS allocates medical care at 6.074% of CPI, yet healthcare spending is 15%+ of GDP. Does BLS believe government and insurance companies pay the balance, so it's "free" to consumers?

Knowing that the initialisms in these sentences stand for the Bureau of Labor Statistics, the Consumer Price Index, and the Gross Domestic Product isn't much help either.

Familiarity with initialisms leads us to see them even where they aren't. In July 2004 an air sickness bag with the letters *BOB* written on it was found in a toilet on a United Airlines flight bound for Los Angeles. The pilot concluded that *BOB* was an initialism for *bomb on board* and turned the plane around. In the end, no bomb was found, and no one could agree as to what *BOB* stood for.

Input is a word popular with POWERPOINT PEOPLE and is often used interchangeably with *feedback*. It is an inhuman way to describe human activities.

> I need everyone's input [opinion].

> Employees will have the opportunity to provide their input [suggestions] on how we can make the company a better place to work.

> New York Stock Exchange chairman and chief executive Dick Grasso says he has no input [say] over his own pay.

Intelligence. In modern English the possession of intelligence does not have to do with smarts, it has to do with surveillance capability. The word, sometimes expanded to *intelligence data*, commonly appears either as a EUPHEMISM for *secrets* or as PRETENTIOUS LANGUAGE for *information*, usually information that somebody doesn't want somebody else to know. *Spying* is *intelligence gathering*, *electronic spying* is *signal intelligence*, and a *spy* is an *intelligence agent*, *intelligence officer*, or *intelligence operative*.

> The funerals have taken place in Spain of seven intelligence agents killed in an ambush in Iraq.

Should federal law enforcement agencies share intelligence data with local law enforcement agencies?

Human intelligence, once seen as something to strive for, is now a euphemism for *spies* and *snitches*.

It was not a lack of legal powers that failed to prevent the terrorist attacks of Sept. 11. It was a lack of human intelligence.

Intelligence is a word popular with businesspeople who view their competitors and their customers as people who must be spied on. This is accomplished by hiring a *competitive intelligence professional*, a euphemism for *business spy*.

As more and more companies recognize the value of keeping tabs on the competition, the importance of the competitive intelligence professional grows.

Interact, interface. *Interact* is a scientific word used to describe, for example, the relationship between plants and microbial pathogens, or the hippocampal-septal axis and gonadal hormones. *Interface* is generally associated with computer connections. They are cold and ill suited to describe communication between people.

A young girl followed us for a ways, obviously eager to interact. But we spoke no Malagasy and she spoke no English.

I have had 12 years of acute care nursing experience and would love to interface with your current primary care provider.

One of the major design objectives was to create in Bank employees the overwhelming urge to interact.

I'M REALLY SLOW ABOUT RESPONDING TO MAIL. I WILL READ ALL MAIL AND RESPOND WHENEVER POSSIBLE. I LOOK FORWARD TO INTERACTING WITH YOU ALL.

What I enjoy in a working environment? I really enjoy interfacing with people.

Invest. Wagering on the outcome of a sporting event is called *gambling*, but wagering on the stock market is called *investing*. The latter gamble, essential to the survival of the world's economic system, is cloaked in a EUPHEMISM to obscure the risk.

Why aren't the investors falling all over themselves to invest in your hot new startup?

Although there's always an element of risk involved with equity investment, our investment process ensures that it's carefully controlled.

See also RISK ADVERSE.

Job Undescription. A growing number of jobs are known by titles that obscure the nature of the work.

administrative associate, administrative professional = secretary
business entrepreneur = businessperson
cash flow broker, secondary lender, subprime lender = loan shark
contingent employee, contract employee = temp
corporate underwriter = advertiser
cybarian, media specialist = librarian
dining room attendant = busboy
fugitive recovery agent = bounty hunter
government affairs strategist = lobbyist
home builder = real estate developer
parking enforcement agent = meter maid
personal assistant = servant
personality = entertainer
policymaker = politician, bureaucrat
tribute artist = impersonator

Knowledge management, knowledge worker. The word *knowledge* is sometimes used in affected terms such as *knowledge leader* and *knowledge report*. And then there is *knowledge management*.

Those who collect and sort information to sell it for money call that information *knowledge*—thus *knowledge management*, a term meant to give a veneer of respectability to their trade.

Knowledge management occasionally appears as an overblown term for *filing*, but more typically it is used to mean 1) pattern recognition or 2) the insane—there is no other word to describe it—belief that all knowledge, including such unquantifiable things as skill, experience, and talent, can be gathered from an organization's workers and then reduced to something akin to software code or mathematical formulae. *Knowledge management* is not about managing information that a business already possesses. It is about obtaining information for the purpose of either selling it or turning it into an algorithm that may be used to replace staff with less-skilled and lower-waged surrogates.

Knowledge management comes with its own subset of prepackaged *knowledge* words. *Knowledge worker* is particularly odious. Here are two definitions of it:

Knowledge Worker. An individual whose primary contribution is through the knowledge that they possess or process. This contrasts with workers whose work is predominantly manual or following highly specified procedures with little scope for individual thought.

Knowledge workers are highly skilled analysts who support complex products or services, while process workers resolve the more redundant requests that have relatively simple answers.

Other terms from the creepy knowledge management lexicon:

knowledge analyst = consultant, project manager
knowledge archaeology = research
knowledge asset = useful information
knowledge audit, knowledge inventory, knowledge mapping =
    learning who knows what (*social network mapping* is learning
    who knows who)
knowledge base = computer-accessible archive
knowledge broker = salesperson
knowledge café = meeting room, online chat room
knowledge capital = skills, know-how
knowledge capture = recording every activity of and scrap of
    writing produced by workers
knowledge center = library
knowledge codification = data entry
knowledge commercialization = selling information
knowledge cycle = discovering and sharing information
knowledge economy = information business

knowledge elicitation = asking workers to chronicle everything
that they do
knowledge narrative = sales pitch
knowledge networking = sharing information
knowledge object = available fact
knowledge product = information for sale
knowledge provider = store
knowledge recipe = formula
knowledge refining = sorting information
knowledge repository = library, memo, human brain
knowledge seeker = customer
knowledge value chain = how money is made from information
knowledge wrapper = file

Launch. One can launch a boat or a spacecraft or even an attack. But nowadays everything is launched—even people are launched—and very little is introduced, started, begun, or opened, which gives everyday activities an unmerited drama. *Launch* in these uses means execute or implement and is sometimes inflated to *initial launch* and *initial soft launch*.

> We're pleased to announce the initial soft launch of a major new initiative.

> SMS.AC MAKES HISTORY WITH MOST
> SUCCESSFUL PRODUCT LAUNCH EVER

> *Launching Our Black Children for Success* is a groundbreaking book that goes beyond the typical "how to get your kid into the best school or college" advice.

> WCVB Launching New Weekend Newscasts

Leader. Politicians, bosses, and other people in positions of authority like to refer to themselves as *leaders*. A well-funded PR industry aids them in this flattery, and now anyone who gives a speech or attends a conference is called a *leader*. But the commanding influence a *leader* possesses by definition is cheapened by such diffusion.

> If you think small tech business leaders in Texas are satisfied with their ranking as the 5th top region in the U.S. in small tech, think again!

Companies like to confer the title *leader* on their products, although the standard for its conferment—sales? distribution? name recognition?—is even more ambiguous than that for politicians and businesspeople.

> Settle for nothing less than the world leader in nautical toilet designs.

Leftist Language can be divided into three categories: politics, new age, and therapy. Most of it is so gray and pithless that it is sometimes borrowed by the Right to further its own ends. New age and therapy words in particular are popular with 1) self-improvement crooks, 2) sellers of bogus medical products, and 3) corporations, who use them in their newsletters in an attempt to appear as if they care about their workers.

Politics

at risk = vulnerable
diversity = minorities
empower = help
empowered = powerful

enslaved people = slaves
imperialism, interventionism = meddling, interference
limited English proficient person = does not speak English
movement = cause
raise awareness of = publicize
same-sex = homosexual
solidarity = unity
undocumented worker = illegal alien
uprising = riot

New Age

achieve balance = be fair
alignment = harmony
celebrate = recognize
consciousness = perception, insight
holistic = broad, complete
a life-enriching experience = inspiring
organic = a good fit
well-being = health

Therapy

achieve closure = complete
closure = a conclusion
companion animal = pet
conflict resolution = peace
conflicted = uncertain
consensus building = cooperation
dialogue = discussion
dysfunctional = sick, flawed
egocentric = selfish

embrace = accept
enablement = helping yourself
I feel conflicted = I can't decide
intervention = guidance
self-actualized = complete, satisfied
self-aware, self-centered = selfish
self-directed = independent
socially engaged = neighborly
time-out = a pause, a discussion

Liberal has become the *commie* of the early twenty-first century. It is a word that turns human beings into alien creatures and it serves as a powerful term of political opprobrium. Conservative polemicists use it to mean radical or appeaser or loser or pretty much any unattractive quality that one can imagine. Not even liberals like to call themselves *liberal* any more, preferring the word *progressive*.

Americans need to be reminded about the outrageous actions of the liberals during the Cold War as the same liberals make similar arguments regarding the war on terrorism.

Limbaugh exposes the farce of liberal "tolerance" and reveals the true agenda of liberals who misuse the law to force Christianity out of the public square.

From pandering to Hollywood to slandering the right, Liberals seem to say the craziest things.

Link calls to mind a chain, steel bonds, undeniable connection. It is much stronger to say that X and Y are *linked* than to say that they have a casual association, or that they inhabit the same part of the world, or that they have mutual interests (although those interests are not necessarily of any particular significance).

> President Bush spent Wednesday trying to draw a link between a possible war in Iraq and the war against terrorism. He repeated accusations that Iraq is linked to the al Qaeda terrorist network.

> There is an undeniable link between acts of terror and illicit drugs.

The feebleness of *link* has spawned *close link* and the more emphatic *direct link*. But in their effort to narrow the definition of *link*, they merely reveal its weakness.

> Saddam Hussein had links to al Qaeda, links to terrorism. But we have never claimed that he had a direct link to the September 11th events.

When a link is shown to be made of hot air, not iron, those who once favored the word sever their link to *link*. The message is unchanged, but by using a different word it is hoped that we won't notice.

> "The reason I keep insisting that there was a relationship between Iraq and Saddam and al Qaeda [is] because there was a relationship between Iraq and al Qaeda," Bush said.

Looking-Glass Language. Enron's *document retention policy* was in fact its document *destruction* policy. That is Looking-Glass Language, the brazen declaration that black is white, when, for example, *clarify* is used in place of *obscure* or when *share* is used in place of *sell*.

> We may share any of the personal information that we collect about you with companies or other organizations outside the Bank One family.

> Unlike the bill that passed the Democrat-controlled Senate last year, this year's bill will not impose unrealistic fuel efficiency standards on automobiles.

> BALANCED ENERGY POLICY SHOULD EMPHASIZE COAL

> The president also vowed to protect small business owners from being taxed twice through the unfair death tax.

> Since Iraq's liberation, the dominant theme of Western news reporting has been the guerrilla attacks against U.S. troops.

Loyalty vs. **loyalists.** Loyalty between friends is considered admirable. Corporations consider it an equally admirable trait when the object of one's loyalty is their product.

> Minorities, he said, have more than 20 percent of the disposable income in the United States, they have good brand loyalty, and their numbers are growing.

Win over your existing patrons with a customer loyalty program, and watch sales reach new heights.

Loyalty is clearly important. Rather, the key point is that loyalty must be managed correctly.

To be a *loyalist*, however, is to be a fanatic.

President Bush blamed Saddam Hussein loyalists and what he called foreign terrorists for the latest wave of attacks in Iraq.

The word *loyalist* is sometimes extended to *loyalist elements*, a doubly bad thing.

Manage, Management. There is an abundance of things that require management in our complex times; we are told that we need to manage our debt, our risk, our disease, our finances, our energy expenses, our health care costs. Those who lose their temper are sent to *anger management* classes; those who work too much attend *stress management* seminars.

The constant demand for management in our lives implies that things are out of control.

> Any powerful new technology needs to be properly managed or else terrible consequences could occur.

> You still must have your head in the right place regarding money management. If not, a bad streak can wipe you out.

> While this is painful, it is manageable—and it must be managed, or else we court disaster.

Manipulative modifiers are words or prefixes used to make bad things look good by transforming good things into bad. *Equality*, for example, is modified into the term *relative equality*, which is *inequality*. Other examples are similarly loathsome.

> *adult literature* = pornography
> *chocolatey cookies* = cookies with no chocolate
> *creation science* = biblical myth
> *disbeneficiaries* = casualties, victims
> *golden dollar* = gold-colored coin with no gold
> *guided democracy* = dictatorship
> *information management* = censorship
> *limited sovereignty* = no meaningful control
> *mass customization* = mass production
> *negative growth* = decline, loss
> *nonauthentic, nonfunctional, nongenuine* = fake, imitation
> *nondisclosure* = secrecy
> *political education* = brainwashing
> *scientific palmistry* = fortune-telling
> *semipermanent* = temporary
> *suboptimal* = bad
> *thick shake* = milk shake with no milk
> *war normal* = abnormal

Matrix is one of the most popular GROOVY LINGO words. It means, in unaffected English, a mold or a grid. In the first example below, it refers to an outline; in the second, a chart.

> The following matrix clearly illustrates the manner in which the required coursework meets the requirements for certification to teach secondary English in Missouri.

The Pentagon's Arabic Media and Programs Unit has developed a "truth matrix" of allegedly unfair or untrue reports.

Measurable, Measurability. Ours is a world of pie charts and spreadsheets, where things must be measurable to be trusted. To apply the standard of measurability to opinions, ideas, ideals, beliefs, emotions, and ethics is crazy, but people are leery of what cannot be quantified. Measurability has become a goal unto itself.

Love is concrete, measurable behavior and action that demonstrates to your partner and the whole world that you respect and care for this person.

A near-total absence of research and measurability are badly undermining U.S. attempts to bolster its image via public diplomacy in Muslim countries.

Make Success Measurable!: A Mindbook-Workbook for Setting Goals and Taking Action

The cloning of embryos for medical purposes generates roughly the same arguments as does abortion—the measurability, or non-measurability, of worth in a specific life.

If my love for God is measurable in the human relationships around me, I must therefore assume that my "like" for God is similarly measurable.

The measured use of force is a fair minded–sounding EUPHE-MISM coined to make palatable the bloody truths of bombing or killing people. It insulates us from the facts and can make offensive warfare appear to be defensive or even magnanimous.

He argued that sometimes the measured use of force was the only way to stop the world from being enveloped by chaos and violence.

We should be exporting peace and prosperity and leading the world in the measured use of force, since we are one of the handful of nations well-armed enough to have that luxury.

Medication and its friendly sounding truncation, *meds*, are EUPHEMISMS to disguise the uncomfortable truth that many of us are on drugs.

My very bright seventh-grader is on medication for attentional difficulties.

Timing Is Everything: Implantable polymer chip delivers meds on schedule.

You can order anti-depressants, weight loss meds, and pain relief meds online with NO PRESCRIPTION.

Meme was coined to mean a thought or belief or behavior that can spread from person to person within a culture. Outside of academia, however, it is almost always used as PRETENTIOUS LANGUAGE for *idea*, *slogan*, and so on.

I am utterly enthralled and enchanted with your new meme.

Government prohibition of meme-spreading of harmful products is far less intrusive than laws against self-destructive behavior itself.

The hijackers' brains, for example, no longer exist, but the meme that killed them—the meme of fundamentalist hatred—is doing quite well.

Mission. Once upon a time only warriors and religious propagandists defined their tasks as *missions*. Now everyone does. Admittedly, it is impressive to read:

> Our mission is to conserve Earth's living heritage, our global biodiversity, and to demonstrate that human societies are able to live harmoniously with nature.

But *mission* is a bombastic word when used in contexts involving pedestrian matters.

> OUR MISSION! The purpose of this site is to support and promote drag racing of pickups and my Dri Wash business.

> Our mission is to promote social development, physical fitness, discipline & leadership through the sport of competitive cheerleading.

> Our mission is to provide our valued customers with the finest portable bathroom and shower facilities available.

> Our Mission. Consistently satisfying the expectations of our consumers, customers, employees, and stockholders by producing and selling quality snacks.

Corporate goals are often described in a pretentious *mission statement*, the written form of the equally pretentious *strategic vision*. Companies also compose *vision statements* and *value statements*, which are the same as *mission statements*.

Modalities has long been favored by the medical profession and academia, where it serves as technical jargon for what the rest of the English-speaking world calls *approaches* or *techniques*. But *modalities* has been discovered by new age "therapists" and bureaucrats are warming to it as well.

How Crystals & Other Energy Modalities Work

Be prepared to experience story-telling and mask making as well as many other expressive arts modalities.

SOME SUGGESTIONS FOR MODALITIES IN AGRICULTURE NEGOTIATIONS

Mode is popularly attached to a number of ordinary human activities to make them sound less ordinary.

I think its because when girls are not sleeping, they're in shopping mode! Where as when men are not sleeping, they're in SEX mode!

Many women have told me they refuse to date a man who smells like a cigarette and tastes, in kissing mode, like an ashtray.

Be aware that we are in potty training mode, so the laundry is not always so pleasant a chore.

Mongrels. There is a linguistic category known as portmanteaus, which are words formed by fusing two or more distinct words. *Brunch*, for example, is a portmanteau combining *breakfast* and *lunch*.

Mongrels are created in the same way but for the purpose of disguise. Few would try to get away with calling entertainment *education*, thus *edutainment* was born.

advermation = advertisement
advertorial = advertisement
coopetition = competition
cosmeceuticals = pharmaceuticals [drugs]
edutainment = entertainment
infomercial = commercial
infotainment = entertainment
infotisement = advertisement
journolobbyist = lobbyist
merchantainer = merchant [salesperson]
merchantainment = merchandising [selling]
nutraceuticals = pharmaceuticals [drugs]
retailtainment = retailing [selling]
shoppertainment = shopping [selling]

National security. Many unsavory acts are committed in the name of national security. We usually accept it as a rationale because we interpret SECURITY to mean safety, and because we tie the safety of the nation to our personal safety. One cannot help but wonder, however, why our safety should so frequently involve acts of injustice.

> President Bush issued guidelines banning racial profiling except in cases of terrorism and national security.

> Survivors of the crew tried to sue defense contractors, alleging defects in the ship's defense systems, but the government blocked them on the basis of national security.

Natural and **all-natural** are WEASEL WORDS that when applied to a product don't necessarily mean what they appear to. They suggest that the product contains nothing artificial or synthetic. But there is no FDA regulation limiting the use of these advertising terms. *Natural* and *all-natural* are also equated with *healthy* and *safe*, but arsenic, anthrax, and E. coli are natural too.

Blue Energy is natural energy, using only natural flavors, natural caffeine and a special proprietary energy blend to safely give you that extra edge!

Learn about natural supplements and products for weight loss, including hydroxycitric acids, ephedra, gugulipid, medium chain triglycerides....

The dessert pizza crumb topping contains milk, mono- and diglycerides, and natural flavor.

Next-generation. Where we once were proud to have our products and gadgets be *state-of-the-art,* now we expect nothing less than *next-generation.* While it suggests exciting parallels to *Star Trek,* the expression *next-generation* describes things that are nothing more than new.

Next-generation DVD standard to hold five times more data

Kaiser has hundreds of medical offices and hospitals and thought it might have to replace many of them with expensive next-generation buildings.

AOL readies next-generation service

Next-generation banking solutions from HP Services enable you to transform your organization into a more service-centric structure.

Nuanced is a chic way to say *subtle.* But *nuanced* itself has become more nuanced, and it now substitutes for a host of other words.

The need is for nuanced [subtle] diplomacy that reconciles several interests, rather than obvious decisions.

He also gives a nuanced [thoughtful] appraisal of the Cold War, demonstrating that it was not as important as popularly believed in determining U.S. behavior in Africa.

The reality of this country is much more nuanced [complex] than this black-versus-white, good-region-versus-evil-region perception.

Asia, Europe give nuanced [cool] welcome to Bush's space dream.

Our high quality black inkjet cartridge delivers sharp black text, rich gray tones, and perfectly nuanced [shaded] halftones.

Padding adds nothing except length to a sentence. It is surprisingly difficult to excise it. Some of the hundreds of examples:

as I mentioned earlier
as they say
at the end of the day
at this point in time
based in large part on
beyond a shadow of a doubt
by and large
I would certainly think that
in a sense
in any case
if you will
in a way
in actual fact
in terms of
in the context of
in the most basic sense
in the process of
in the same vein

interestingly enough
it is an absolute fact that
it is obvious that
it seems as if
let me begin by pointing out
needless to say
nothing less than
such factors as
the bottom line is
the fact of the matter is that
the reality of the situation is that
the very epitome of
there's absolutely no question that
to say the least
to the extent that
when all is said and done

Paradigm and **paradigmatic** are florid words signaling pompousness. *Paradigm* is the favored PRETENTIOUS LANGUAGE for *approach* and *model*, while *paradigmatic* substitutes for *consummate* and *ideal*.

Do IT Professionals Need College Degrees? We need a new paradigm.

From my perspective, Mack Sennett is as much the paradigmatic Hollywood Director as D. W. Griffith.

Paradigm and *paradigmatic* are habitual among POWERPOINT PEOPLE, whose prose often is tangled to the point of incoherence.

We will now consider the paradigmatic aspects of the meme concept, for they have relevance to the acceptance, or non-acceptance, of the future scenario.

A shared commitment to a paradigm ensures that its practitioners engage in the paradigmatic observations that its own paradigm can do most to explain.

Physical, applied to competitive sport, gives us a socially acceptable way to say *violent.*

> Hockey is a physical sport.

Piracy is a scary word used to describe the act of copying material from the Internet—an activity whose ethical and legal parameters are far from clear. Those who feel uncomfortable calling it *stealing* should not use *piracy*, either. The neutral phrase is, simply, *copying*; the use of *piracy* has been fostered by industries that consider the activity to result in lost profits.

> The impact of online piracy on the U.S. music business has been "devastating," says the head of the Recording Industry Association of America, Cary Sherman.

> The U.S. recording industry has sued a further 477 people for online copyright infringement as part of its effort to stop music piracy.

> New Website Teaches Kids That Music Piracy Is Wrong

PowerPoint People. It is freakish to call paper *fiber media*, or a plan a *progress and action structure*. Such language has to be trained into an adult, nurtured in surroundings barren of natural English, encouraged by like-minded people. The product of such training is a PowerPoint Person.

PowerPoint People gather in places such as regional business conferences and motivational seminars. They often have advanced degrees in specialties such as Behavior Finance Theory, Biomedical Reengineering, and Marketing Process Management. Their jargon isn't simply corporate or scholarly abstraction, and it isn't used for effect or camouflage. PowerPoint People write and speak their smorgasbord of GROOVY LINGO, COMPUTER LANGUAGE, and HACKNEYED EXPRESSIONS because it has become natural to them.

PowerPoint People write sentences such as these:

> Thus a more realistic assumption of a spatially varying cropping pattern and an alternative definition of equity by giving priority for assured water supply in the two seasons would have had better implementability.

> We are internalizing their methodology to build our own culture of innovation.

> As they value each other's differences, open themselves to new possibilities, practice Think Win-Win, and build trust, they reap the benefits of synergizing.

> There is not one book that comes close to impacting and exciting me to the magnitude that yours has. It has crystallized my thinking about how to move my business to the next level, transformed how I approach my clients, and revolutionized

how I leverage my most important assets—my time, talents and money—for maximum results.

Because so many of us are exposed to PowerPoint People, their lingo and phrasing are seeping into everyday language.

Oh, come now. With regard to dealing with a woman of substance, that mode of response [reaction] is pitifully outdated and you know better, really.

Here are some simple examples on how to visually eyeball [estimate] your food portions by comparing them to the size of everyday items.

Thank you for the grandest and most cost-effective [thrifty] vacation I have ever experienced.

There are so many action items [things to do] and improvement activities [projects] on everyone's "to-do" list nowadays.

Here's an interesting factoid [fact].

In reviewing the new slate of Grand Lodge members, I think this is an extremely positive situation [great].

By the middle of the second semester, I was completely integrated into [part of] the class.

I cohabitate with [live with] my boyfriend of six years and we have an adorable three-year-old son named AJ.

It sounded like a really good value proposition [idea].

But when you get really task saturated [overworked], you aren't able to do as good a job.

My advice on creatine would be try it when you're not in a pressurized situation [tense].

I've checked out many mousing surface solutions [mouse pads] from many different companies.

We're a dual-professional couple [we both work].

Pre- is a prefix with opposite meanings, which leads to confusion and exploitation. *Pre-* is commonly a truncation of *previously*, a synonym for *already*, as in *preowned* and *preassembled*. When we receive a letter bestowing the good news that we have been *preapproved* for a credit card or *prequalified* for a loan and asking us for personal information, we take it to mean we are already approved or qualified. But *pre-* also means prior to or not yet, as in *preelection* and *prehistoric*. In junk mail, being *preapproved* means that you are in a state of not yet having been approved and that you are being given an application for consideration for approval. Thus your personal information is extracted, which can be used or sold by a junk-mailer in whatever way it wishes and, more to the point, may or may not lead to an approval. One can no more be preapproved than one can be predead.

Pre-'s opposite meanings often lead to ambiguous sentences, such as *Enter our raffle with confidence because the winning numbers are pre-selected at random by computer.*

Pre- is also used extraneously. To invite first-class passengers to *preboard* an aircraft is to invite them to get on before they get on. To *preplan* a meeting is similarly absurd, as is the now idiomatic *prefabricate*.

Preemption means to shoot first and ask questions later. It attained prominence in September 2002 when the Bush administration's approach to international relations, labeled a *preemption doctrine* by the media, was published in a document titled *The National Security Strategy of the United States of America*:

> The United States has long maintained the option of preemptive actions to counter a sufficient threat to our national security... To forestall or prevent such hostile acts by our adversaries, the United States will, if necessary, act preemptively.

Preempt, preemption, acting preemptively, preemptive strike, preemptive measures, preemptive military action—all are EUPHEMISMS for *attacking, bombing, invading,* and *war.*

> We simply do not know enough to be able to preempt with confidence.

> He has weapons of mass destruction. The lesser risk is in pre-emption. We've got to stop wishing away the problem.

> Do we wait for Saddam and hope he doesn't do what we know he is capable of, or do we take some preemptive action?

> The doctrine of preemption is a rational and appropriate response to a world of very new and dangerous threats.

The Japanese bombing of Pearl Harbor, where America was building up its Pacific fleet, was an example of preemption, although from our vantage point it was a *sneak attack.*

Pretentious Language. Certain words and terms have an air of snobbery. They are not devious; they are just phony. Some, such as *distinguished career* and *informed sources*, are used in references only to the social and political elite.

academy = school
aficionado, maven = fan
assiduously = hard
bifurcated = divided
cleanse = clean
cleansing bar = soap
converse = talk
counterintuitive = nonsense
denouement = end
discontinuity = conflict
disingenuous = misleading
dissemble = confuse
distinguished = respectable
efficacious = effective
egress = exit
envisioneer = visionary
governance = governing, government
hegemony = dominance, supremacy, mastery
institution of higher learning, postsecondary institution = college,
    university
landmark = important
oeuvre = life's work
opaque =hidden
paradigm = model
persona = image

postmodern = contemporary
prestigious = famous
procure = purchase, buy, get
refute = deny
skilled artisan = worker, craftsperson
staffers = workers
timepiece = watch
trepidatious = nervous
tutelage = training, schooling
visage = face

Proact. People who anticipate situations, who don't just react but take charge—these are the people we admire. Logic would have it that they would be said to *preact*. Instead we have the freak ATROCITY *proact*.

> Leaders need to proact and prepare the organization to be responsive to a changing market environment.

Proact is sometimes used like *preempt*: attack first.

> We must be vigilant and ready with an action plan to deal with the attacks as they come and they will. We must proact where possible.

Problem. Although the world may be beset with problems, our lexicon no longer has them. Instead, we have *challenges, conditions, areas of concern, developments, difficulties, downsides, adverse effects,* *glitches, issues, improvement opportunities, learning opportunities, setbacks, situations, trouble areas,* and *vulnerabilities.* Nowadays we apparently would rather seize an opportunity than fix a problem.

Similar words on the way out include *mistake,* which is being replaced by *anomaly, error,* and *inaccuracy;* and *bad,* replaced by *challenging, faulty,* and *not optimal.*

Product is turning up behind names of products for no apparent reason.

It is actually quite impressive how the Penders family developed this amazing "one size fits all" hair rinse product.

When considering a colon cleanser product there are many health supplements from which to choose.

Every month we feature a different author, publisher or book product who has earned the RLK! seal of approval!

The MEDICOTT covers are machine washable. Never wash the pillow product itself.

This product is brewed with wheat, barley, spices, and ale yeast to produce a delicious beer product that will be enjoyed by almost anyone.

See also COMFORT WORDS.

Professional. To be a *professional* means possessing a high standard of knowledge and expertise acquired through rigorous education, intensive training, and diligent work. The word is thus a good one to be associated with, and now everyone wants to be known as a *professional*. Plumbers are *plumbing professionals*, businesspeople are *business professionals*, real estate agents are *real estate professionals*, and so on. Less specific kinds of professionals also abound, including *career professionals*, *industry professionals*, *knowledgeable professionals*, *seasoned professionals*, and *true professionals*.

Public relations, a EUPHEMISM for *propaganda*, is so firmly established that it would be shocking to see it replaced by the word that it masks.

> She is a TCU cheerleader and member of Chi Omega. After graduation, Lindsay would like to pursue a career in [propaganda] for a professional sports team.

> Sponsoring charity organizations, tournaments and other functions is a useful [propaganda] tool.

Quality of life is a cliché that is meant to convey a broad set of unquantifiable states of being, such as contentment, happiness, health, and anything else one cares to throw in.

Assessing a pet's quality of life is an ongoing process, not a one-time decision.

Quality of life is often cited in evaluations of the merits of particular locations, but it is so hazy that it can mean anything from a low crime rate to clean sidewalks.

Canada always ranks high in any international quality of life assessment.

Florida's Great Northwest has the special gifts that mean quality of life for those lucky enough to live in this special place.

Quality of life is often used where the simple word *life* says it all.

People who work excessively long hours are dissatisfied with the overall quality of their lives—regardless of whether or not they have children.

Real, Really, Truly. Used in advertising to hype dubious claims, *real*, *really*, and *truly* carry the tinge of desperation.

"This is a real breakthrough in videoconferencing," said Eli Doron, CTO of RADVISION.

Mailinator: A Truly New and Slick Email Concept.

Compared to the standard all-metal peelers of yesterday, this is a really superior product.

Reasonable. What is reasonable? It depends.

No reasonable offer refused!

We recycle waste whenever it is reasonable to do.

Most reasonable citizens don't have a problem providing their names when pawning or purchasing a handgun.

Despite outcries from civil libertarians, Cheney called the tribunals a "perfectly reasonable and responsible way to go," given the nature of the terrorist threat.

Redundancies

a high standard of excellence
alcohol-related drunk driving
all the way through
always consistent
ATM machine
bonded together
bottom line objective
brand identity
center median
central hub
core nucleus
done deal
emblematic logo
end result
energy drive
factually accurate
forecast the future
foreign imports
free gift
gathered together
hilariously funny
HIV virus
hot-water heater
important watershed
individually designed to meet your needs
information source
inquisitive curiosity
IRA account

located on

matched pair

narrow self-interest

past experience

past history

possible alternatives

prior planning

proven track record

regal palace

SAT test

secure together

situated in

some additional

specially tailored

surrounding environs

terrible tragedy

time period

toll charges

torrential downpour

the torso from the neck down

true facts

unprecedented new

viable alternative

visual depiction

Regime is a pejorative label that governments apply to other governments they oppose.

Iraqi Regime Collapses, Baghdad Under U.S. Control

North Korean regime balks at continued negotiations

Syrian Regime: A Bitter enemy of Internet

UNESCO Award to Librarian/Journalist Angers Cuban Regime

U.S. Could Change Iranian Regime without a Single Shot, Expert Says

Regime change is a EUPHEMISM for *coup* or *overthrow*.

Resonance resonates with importance more than *importance* does.

This is interesting, but given some of the recent comments in the press it takes on greater resonance.

To *resonate with* likewise sounds sexier than to *interest* or *appeal to*.

This solution did not resonate with the average consumer.

We want to present issues that may resonate with students transitioning into a new environment.

Risk adverse. When people use *risk adverse*, they intend to say *risk averse*. A person feels *averse*; an outcome is *adverse*.

Are they a risk-taker or are they risk-adverse?

Most investment advisors are in agreement that it is more accurate to think of investors as typically being loss adverse rather than risk adverse.

Used to describe a disinclination to INVEST money, *risk adverse* is a term of dubious merit even when the correct word, *averse*, is used. This mechanical expression conceals that to invest is to put money in jeopardy; what's more, it has come to be used pejoratively, synonymous with *timid* and *spineless*. The philosophy expressed in the maxim *better safe than sorry* is no longer seen as a virtue.

I have been uncomfortable with the way risk is generally discussed and approached, and have the nagging belief that our society has become very risk adverse with potentially dire social consequences.

NASA is too old, too bureaucratic, and too risk adverse.

Education of the household head is found to decrease risk-aversion.

Rogue state, rogue nation. Every country, including the United States, violates international law when it serves its interest to do so. When countries that we view as enemies do it, we call them rogues.

Our nation must adopt a "rogue nation regime change war policy" in an attempt to keep the battlefront on foreign soil.

The UN has proven itself not merely irrelevant, but a growing threat to the international interests of the United States in a world of rogue nation-states and shadowy international movements whose purpose is to destroy this nation.

Say It Again. When users of GROOVY LINGO, PRETENTIOUS LANGUAGE, and the like lose confidence in their preferred manner of speech, they tack on a plain English decoder.

"This is our opportunity to *differentiate our brand,* to tell customers what makes our stores different, better, and special," Spinozzi said.

Conscious choice can only take place for those who are willing to challenge their *paradigms,* what they believe to be true.

Education reform is *sweat equity;* it's hard to accomplish.

"Many are spending half their resources on *reactive solutions,*" Thompson said, "fixing things that are already broken. We need to get people out of *the fire drill mode.*"

Cambridge Advisors are the pioneers of *holistic* financial planning—planning that focuses on the person, not a product.

When kids get picked on, they may *take it to the next level.* They may seek protection from an illegal street gang.

One thing is certain. President/general manager Dave Dombrowski will not *be a bow on somebody else's fiddle*. He won't allow himself or his team to be used in a bidding game.

Departments will determine *what level of granularity is used*, i.e. at what level information resources will be described.

Many LD children lack the ability for *revisualization*. That is, the child is unable to remember a mental picture of the things she has seen or learned before.

Fully functional book. Has all pages.

Security. A society in which *security* is an inescapable word is not doing well. Ours has security codes in doors, security checkpoints at airports, security patches on Internet browsers, security settings in computer operating systems, security features in paper money. What is meant by *security* is never clearly stated— privacy? safety? censorship?—but we have to have it.

"People are cutting back just about everywhere," one vendor representative told me, "but they're definitely willing to pay for security."

Students in urban residences need security shuttle service.

Tommy G. Thompson today announced the issuance of two Food and Drug Administration regulations that will bolster the safety and security of America's food supply.

Wireless computer networks pose a threat to the security of anyone using them, warn security experts.

Parents can rely on all of AOL's built-in safety and security features to keep their teens safe.

The security fence, the separation barrier, the terrorism prevention fence. What, exactly, is the thing that Israel has built to keep out the Palestinians? It looks like the Berlin Wall—concrete topped by coils of razor wire. The Berlin Wall was called a *wall*. But the Israeli government didn't want to call their wall a *wall* because that would remind people of the Berlin Wall. So the government instead called it the *security fence*. This didn't work, since everyone could see that it was a wall, not a fence, so the government changed the name to the *separation barrier*. That too, however, was still not quite right. The Israeli government wanted people not just to accept the wall; they wanted them to *like* the wall. So the name has been changed again, to the *terrorism prevention fence*.

Shock and awe is a slogan that removes us from the physical fact of heavy bombing by describing only its emotional effect. A fairer description using the same tactic would be *terror bombing*.

The speed with which *shock and awe* has been adapted to other purposes shows that, while it may have been a bust as a war strategy, it has triumphed as a HACKNEYED EXPRESSION.

Careful planning will, even in times of unpredictable weather, enable you to shock and awe your pals with a quick, tasty steak.

Shock and Awe of Childhood Flu Inspires Parental Love

Explod 6 x 9" 2-Way Car Speakers (pair)—XS-W6921 for $79.99. Shock and awe your passengers with these robust ovals in your rear deck.

A great way to shock and awe your Mom might be to put away clean dishes one day while she's not around, or to load the dishwasher.

Days of Shock and Awe About to Hit the Natural Gas and Power Markets

Parenting is war, ladies and gentlemen, and if you're not prepared to shock and awe your kids into being creative, well-mannered, behaved individuals, then don't have them in the first place.

Sticker Shock and Awe

Simply should be reserved for actions that are simple.

If your skills are more strongly musical then feel free to simply compose 10 songs about the powers of the wind listed below.

Simply reconstitute a functional Tn5 transposition system by combining transposase, "transposon" (any DNA sequence of interest contained between the two 19 bp Tn5 transposase recognition sequences), target DNA (e.g., plasmid, cosmid, or BAC clone) and a $Mg2+$-containing buffer in a tube and incubate at 37°C.

The best way to eliminate this smoke is by either going outside or, better yet, to simply stop smoking.

Why cannot you simply take what is good in Christianity, what you can define as valuable, what you can comprehend, and leave all the rest, all the absolute dogmas that are in their nature incomprehensible?

Spam and Telemarketing Terminology is designed to shield the perpetrators of these modern-day plagues from the odiousness of their work and may even enable them to fool themselves as they fool others.

junk mail
courtesy offer, direct mail, mailings, marketing letter, marketing mail, reminder card, special offer

pyramid scam
affiliate program, direct marketing, gifting club, multilevel marketing, MLM, network marketing program, program

spam
bulk e-mail, direct marketing, e-mail broadcasts, e-mail campaigns, e-mail marketing, e-mail notices, e-mail offers, interactive advertisement, Internet marketing, invitation letters, invite-a-friend e-mails, marketing e-zine, network marketing, new product alert, a professional communication, push content, remote control selling, targeted e-mail, targeted optformail, tell-a-friend e-mails, unsolicited commercial e-mail, viral e-mail marketing

spammer, telemarketer
e-mail publisher, network marketing business, network marketing company

telemarketing
direct sales, network marketing, teleservices

other
advanced programming [spam tv], courtesy call [unsolicited sales call], downline, franchisee [pyramid scam prey], interstitials [pop-up ads], the warm market [friends, family, and acquaintances of a pyramid scammer], searching for cooperation partners [spamming]

Stakeholder gives the appearance of identifying someone as important or powerful—I am a stakeholder!—but it is just GROOVY LINGO for *interested party* or *employee*. The definition of *stakeholder* is a person to whom the stakes in a wager between other people are entrusted. A stakeholder is not a participant—and thus has literally nothing at stake.

Consider issues like: the project's benefit(s) to the stakeholder; the changes that the project might require the stakeholder to make; and the project activities that might cause damage or conflict for the stakeholder.

Stakeholder interviews are a simple, but very effective mechanism for gaining an understanding of an organization, and for identifying staff needs.

Sticky, stickiness. To refer to a product or to commercial propaganda, particularly Web sites, as *sticky* is to mean that they are attractive or engaging. As their goal, however, is to get their audience hooked, it would be more accurate to say that they are *addictive*.

The application becomes sticky as customers gain a stake in the service and grow reluctant to take their business elsewhere.

DRIVERS OF STICKINESS. In this section we categorize the numerous methods by which companies are attempting to increase their Web site stickiness.

Structural. Disastrous events, according to those in power, are the fault of *structural* problems or of something that is *structurally* out of kilter. Responsibility thus becomes impossible to tack onto any individual or agency and the search for justice can exhaust itself in the labyrinth of *structural reform* and *structural change*.

RICE: In looking back, I believe that the absence of light, so to speak, on what was going on inside the country, the inability to connect the dots, was really structural.

RICE: We had a structural problem in the United States, and that structural problem was that we did not share domestic and foreign intelligence in a way to make a product for policymakers, for good reasons—for legal reasons, for cultural reasons—a product that people could depend upon.

RICE: I fully agree with you that, in hindsight, now looking back, there are many things structurally that were out of kilter. And one reason that we're here is to look at what was out of kilter structurally, to look at what needed to be done, to look at what we already have done, and to see what more we need to do.

RICE: I do not believe that it is a good analysis to go back and assume that somehow maybe we would have gotten lucky by, quote, "shaking the trees." Dick Clarke was shaking the trees, director of central intelligence was shaking the trees, director of the FBI was shaking the trees. We had a structural problem in the United States.

Target, a word that calls to mind the image of a bull's-eye, is a poor choice to use in connection with fluid concepts such as a goal.

> Legislation would target [curtail] violence in video games.

> The administration says it wants to target [earmark] funds to where they're needed most.

> Content-Targeted [matched] Advertising™ is our latest tool for web publishers.

> We finally got some things going our way, being able to bring in a player that we targeted [wanted].

Tasked. When powerful people order other people to do something but don't want to say *ordered*, they use *tasked*.

> I've tasked the Secretary of State to meet with the Secretary General of the United Nations.

The mass media have picked up on the word and now use it just as the powerful people do.

> The rover is tasked with examining Martian rocks and dust for evidence of the past presence of water.

> The envoys are tasked with highlighting the action taken to deal with the Mad Cow outbreak in Washington State.

Taxpayers, used in discussions concerning government revenues, is appropriate. In discussions of more general topics, however, the right word is *citizens*. To generically refer to people as *taxpayers* is to reduce them, often unintentionally, to political passivity.

> As a patriotic American and taxpayer, I do not support President Bush's attempt to settle the old scores of his father.

> The U.S. Taxpayers Party of Michigan stands for Restoration of the United States to "One Nation Under God;" Return to Constitution Government; Stop all Unconstitutional Spending; Protect the Inalienable Right to Life of All (including the unborn); Protect Individual Rights to Keep and Bear Arms; Stop All Unconstitutional Spending; and Comprehensive Immigration Reform. These are only a few of our beliefs.

Terrorism, Terrorist, Terrorize. *Terrorism* and *terrorist* are surprisingly subjective terms. A bloodied nation calls those who attack it *terrorists*, but those who side with the attackers call them *freedom fighters, heroes, martyrs*. When *terrorist* is applied to those who are no more than vandals, activists, or just opponents, and *terrorism* to their activities, the words are stretched beyond acceptable limits.

An arson attack by animal rights terrorists destroyed an unused house at Darley Oaks Farm, where guinea pigs are bred for research.

So don't let the threats and misrepresentations of the anti-spam terrorists frighten you from making a legitimate living on the Internet.

Jack Valenti, chief executive of the Motion Picture Association of America, calls the struggle against unauthorized copying a "terrorist war."

The chairman of American International Group Inc., the world's largest insurer by market value, on Tuesday called lawyers opposed to tort reform "terrorists" and said class-action lawsuits are a "blight" on the United States.

U.S. Education Secretary Rod Paige sparked an uproar when he called the nation's largest teachers' union a "terrorist organization" during a meeting with U.S. governors.

Greenpeace Inc., and other non-exempt Greenpeace entities benefitting from these transfers, have committed numerous acts of eco-terrorism. They have blockaded a U.S. naval base, broken into the central control building of a nuclear power station in England, overrun the Exxon Mobil corporate headquarters in Texas, and rammed a ship into the French sailboat competing in the 2003 America's Cup, permanently damaging the vessel.

One way to reduce the amount of terror in the world is to stop using *terror* and *terrorize* to describe things that are merely frightening or worrisome.

I was terrorized by everyday noises, like planes passing by, thunder, machinery, jackhammers, balloons bursting, and any sudden noise.

Lions' roars terrorize German town

The three incidents had several things in common: all involved stray bullets from gun battles, all terrorized innocent people.

During that time we met others who did not have insurance. We were all terrorized thinking about our kids and wondering if they were going to make it.

Think tank brings to mind the image of a retreat insulated from the world, where minds engage in dispassionate objective research to produce an unbiased analysis. Such, perhaps, was the case when the term for these institutions was first coined in the 1950s, but it is not so now. What occurs at contemporary think tanks is *applied* thinking, that is, thinking toward a goal, and that goal is not impartial. It is rather to provide justification for the political positions of the funders of the think tank. The titles given to think tank spokespeople—*researcher, fellow, analyst*—also mislead, as they call to mind the objectivity of university scholars in organizations where none is wanted. The television commentator or newspaper op-ed writer who is identified as a *fellow* in a *think tank* should more honestly be labeled a *Justification Factory Salesperson*.

Threat. The sole condition necessary for American PREEMPTION, as currently defined, is to claim that something is an imminent, sufficient, or even just an emerging threat. *Threat* is thus a more important word than ever. A *threat* is a menace or a grave danger or, in the confused parlance of politicians, a *grave and growing danger.* It is much more than a *problem,* even a serious one, and it is certainly not the same as a *speculative risk.*

"The insider poses the greatest threat because they know where the most critical information is kept and how to bypass the safeguards on the system," says James Savage, deputy special agent in charge of the Secret Service's financial crimes division.

The threat of forest fires in the East Mountains has been delayed—at least for a little while.

Inspector Findlater said the pig only posed a minor threat to the public if he was "aggravated" or harmed.

It is sad that of all the threats that have come down the pike in the past few years, the one that really *was* a threat—that TER-RORISTS would hijack airliners and fly them into buildings—was ignored and not acted upon. As a result, the government has grown hypersensitive to *threat* and applies the term broadly, to the point of labeling as *possible threats* things that are no more than risks, if even that. Possible threats are now seen everywhere.

The plans involve the use of smallpox vaccine in order to deal with the possible threat of a smallpox outbreak.

U.S. holds Sudanese pilot as possible threat.

Route 53 Tollway Still a Possible Threat to Preserve.

Puerto Rican Terrorists: A Possible Threat to U.S. Energy Installations?

POSSIBLE THREAT TO DRINKING WATER FROM RISING WATER LEVELS IN ABANDONED MINES?

Timeframe. First the word *time* was extended to *time frame. I cannot comment during this time frame.* Now the two words have fused and appear as a single oddity.

We can expect some showers in the afternoon timeframe.

Timeframe is often used as a substitute for *deadline* or *timetable.*

France led objections, calling for a timeframe for the transfer of power from the U.S.-led Coalition Authority to Iraqi civilians.

McDonalds had said that it would cut trans fat in its fries nearly 50 percent by early this year, but now says it has no time frame.

Timeframe is no longer novel enough for some who now substitute the ATROCITY *timezone.*

Blizzard has announced a release timezone, which they think will be Halloween or so.

Totally. This juvenile modifier—*totally cool, totally awesome*—retards the idiom of anyone over the age of sixteen. It is an insatiable parasite. Some of the many words undermined by *totally* are *agree, committed, deadlocked, destroyed, disabled, disagree, disintegrated, drunk, eliminate, free, furnished, new, odorless, original, portable, reliable, safe, silent, understand, understandable, unique,* and *wasted.*

    totally against
    totally amazed
    totally amazing
    totally fucked [up]
    totally involved
    totally pissed off
    totally pleased
    totally professional
    totally redesigned
    totally reliant
    totally satisfying
    totally thrilled
    totally unrealistic

Traction, as a GROOVY LINGO substitute for *appeal, momentum,* or *acceptance,* makes everyone who uses it sound like an ad agency flack or a stockbroker.

> "You need to ask why you've got traction among a certain audience," says Rhett Speros, director of buzz at hot shop Buzztone.

> Ford revival gains traction

The movie's poor revenues suggest that it never got traction, even in regions where "Bible believers" abound.

Perdue got traction from a campaign video he mailed to supporters depicting Barnes as a giant rat destructively swaggering through a cityscape.

Transfer tubes. The bodies of dead soldiers during the Vietnam War were removed from the battlefield in zippered rubber bags that were called *body bags*. The bags did not change, but by the 1991 Gulf War they had become *human remains pouches*. While sounding more clinical, this proved to be too descriptive for those who wished to hide from the consequences of their decisions, and so during the 2003–2004 Iraq War the *body bag* became a *transfer tube*.

Transition is frequently used as a replacement for *move* or CHANGE in both noun and verb forms. The phrase *to transition out* is *to leave*, while *transitioning out of* is *leaving*.

People will remain a priority as the staff, physicians, volunteers and administration transition to the new region.

The transition itself wasn't messy; getting to the point of actually transitioning the company from a public company to a private company was messy.

The rush to finalize a spate of new regulations is a tradition whenever an administration transitions out.

There are several groups of young people transitioning out of foster care who may already be eligible for Medicaid.

Transition is also used as a EUPHEMISM for *firing* people, stressing change and even renewal, like a butterfly emerging from a chrysalis. People who have lost their livelihoods probably don't see it that way.

The primary goal of UnitedRecruiters outplacement is to assist your transitioning employees in successfully re-establishing themselves in new and challenging careers.

Handling transitioning employees with compassion and respect can become an opportunity for business success by preserving employee morale and generating continued goodwill in the community.

See also CRYBABY VERBS.

Ugly Places with Pretty Names

assisted living facility, extended care facility = nursing home
correctional facility, confinement facility = jail, prison
covenant community = commune, hideout
developmental facility = mental hospital
energy center = nuclear power plant
estates, manufactured home community = trailer park
gentlemen's club = strip club
human services = welfare office
individual work space, office space = cubicle
outplacement, career transition services = unemployment office
parking facility = garage
receiving area = loading dock
repository, sanitary landfill = dump
resource recovery facility = garbage incinerator
value retailer = discount store

See also EUPHEMISM AS ART.

Undesirable elements. *Elements* is a word that has come to be applied to groups of people, usually as a deliberate way to transform human beings into objects. The worst elements of all are *undesirable elements.* This phrase was once a EUPHEMISM for racial or religious minorities, but its range has broadened considerably in recent years and now includes just about any group of people that someone can fear or hate.

I have already revealed that I saw that AIDS was man-made to eliminate the undesirable elements of society while I was attached to Naval Security.

Our guests do not have to worry about gawkers and other undesireable elements that a fetish club can attract at times.

It is true that undesirable elements must often be put in their place, and maybe even be put to death if we do not know how to transform and change them.

Undisclosed, used in the expression *undisclosed location,* implies less intrigue than *secret* would, and squelches the impulse people might have to ask questions. Only important people get to hide, or be imprisoned, in an undisclosed location.

The Vice-President, whose visit to Rome is part of a five-day European swing, has spent much of the past two years in undisclosed locations, rarely making public appearances, except at Republican fundraisers.

Today's announcement said only that the former Iraqi dictator would be held at an undisclosed location for the foreseeable future.

Value is an established synonym for the verb *appreciate*, although it can seem obsequious when so used: *We value your input.* As a noun it has for years been used by salespeople who want to persuade prospective customers that a product too costly to be called a BARGAIN is still worth its price. *This car is a real value.*

Value has become a hopeless abstraction, often combined with adjectives that are meant to amplify its power but in fact only make the waters murkier: *absolute value, overall value, real value,* and so on. *Value* implies something good, but that something is never clearly stated.

> I spend most of my time creating and delivering value.

> This repurposeable, leading edge thoughtware delivers results-driven value.

> The mission of your business is to provide a specific Customer Type with a steady stream of Unique Value.

> The newly sophisticated, but still loss adverse, corporate type now accepts that in order to climb up the value chain and thus continually increase customer value they must be willing to give up monopoly technologies and focus on new value.

Value is also seen co-opted in peculiar, often indefinite compounds such as *value-added* [better], *value-based* [smart], *value driver* [benefit], *value proposition* [enticement], and *value-driven* [frugal].

> The present era, the Complexity Era, has a strong focus toward value-based leadership.

> We don't need any more vans coming off the ferries with a month's supply of food staying only at campsites. We need value-added tourism.

> Operationalizing Value Based Management. Understand What Drives Value. Find Where Value Is Created or Destroyed. Make Value the Criterion for Decision-Making. Embed Value into Your Culture.

Value engineering, value management, and *value planning* are all inefficient substitutes for *efficiency.* In modern business jargon they are often EUPHEMISMS for paying fewer people less money to do more work.

Values are subjective—they are not synonymous with virtue or goodness. Hitler had values. Al Qaeda has values.

Many people have a habit of associating their values with a much larger group, which requires prefacing *values* to form, for example, *traditional values, Christian values, American values, family values, community values, civic values,* and *human values.*

Values often change with the passage of time, which can prove awkward. Among the values once included as American were segregation, denying women the vote, and the right to take land away from Native Americans. *Core American values* can mean whatever anybody wants it to mean, but it certainly does not refer to the above historical American values.

> Americans who revere our heritage of freedom and independence must have the courage to defy 1990s political correctness and uphold core American values.

The subjectivity of values is also apparent in the business terms *values-based* and *values-driven*, popular with management consultants, who say that the most efficient businesses are those in which everyone shares the same values. Enron's executives, for example, shared the same values.

> Values-Based Hiring allows an organization to determine whether someone is a cultural fit by asking, "Do the values reflected in an individual's behavior match the desired behavior that is representative of the organization's values?"

Verbal Prestidigitation. Like a magician, those skilled in a certain branch of the rhetorical arts use feints and deception to get their audiences to hear things that were not said and see things that were not written. On May 1, 2003, George W. Bush, costumed in a figher pilot's jumpsuit, stood before a large banner on which were emblazoned the words *Mission Accomplished* and declared an end to *major combat operations* in Iraq.

Major combat operations in Iraq have ended. In the battle of Iraq, the United States and our allies have prevailed.

It was assumed that *major combat operations* was just a fancy way to say *the war.* When it later became clear that the war hadn't ended and was continuing to cost billions of dollars, hundreds of American lives, and thousands of Iraqi lives, President Bush was asked by a reporter if he wanted to retract his statement that the war was over. The president replied that he had never said that the *war* was over, just the *major combat operations.*

Everyone, including U.S. presidents, once felt duty bound to make their communication clear to all. Today, however, comprehensibility is not necessarily the goal. The most egregious instances of Verbal Prestidigitation are, like President Bush's announcement, cunning arrangements of seemingly beneficent words that form skillful hedges. Like the reporter who "misunderstood" *major combat operations,* we cannot bring ourselves to believe that what we heard is not what is meant and so we unwittingly make false sense of a duplicitous statement—usually to our disadvantage.

Viral. Modern salespeople, ever looking on the bright side of things, have found the good in viral activity.

Adding a viral component to an email marketing campaign can really boost response rates.

Reseller licensing of the e-book product—or allowing those who buy the books to "give" them away—adds another viral layer to the promotion.

Viral marketing has proven itself to be an effective marketing communications weapon.

As one sales enthusiast described it, "In the same way that the common cold spreads through sneezes, coughs, and handshakes, your offer now spreads through e-cards, electronic coupons, and invite-a-friend e-mails." As with a virus, this spread occurs without the host's consent—often through an unseen plundering of the host's e-mail address book—although that method of contagion is downplayed. Unlike a virus, however, this infection is spread deliberately. It is an insult to viruses everywhere.

Once you promote your Virtual Stampede system past a certain stage, it will continue to grow by itself, with no further promotion by you! This is the beauty of Viral Marketing.

Vision is used nowadays as a substitute for *goal* or *plan*, or to give a high gloss to things that are really just ideas.

View the architect's groundbreaking vision of our bayfront!

To successfully reconstruct Iraq, it is necessary to provide the Iraqi people with a concrete vision as well as hope for their future.

Going online in June of 2000, the website wowed readers with a groundbreaking vision that broke all the rules and set a new design trend in author sites.

What will Bush's space vision cost?

RAYMOND FLOYD DETAILS HIS GROUND-
BREAKING VISION OF HOW TO PLAY THE GAME
OF GOLF IN HIS WONDERFULLY INSIGHTFUL
BOOK.

Visioning, an ATROCITY, is substituted for *planning* and *foresight*.
It also appears as an adjective in such awkward REDUNDANCIES as
visioning plans, *visioning forums*, and *visioning steering committees*.

Visioning is a planning tool to learn and think about events
that could happen in the future before they occur.

Strategic Visioning Necessary for Survival of the Texas
Produce Industry

After reviewing all input, the Visioning Steering
Committee put East End Beautification as their lead project
for Spring 2002 through 2003.

Visionary. There was a day when only crazy people or biblical
prophets had visions. Now business executives and politicians
have visions every day. Products and companies do too.

Bottom line, this is definitely more than a phone. The 7110
is a visionary product that caters to a whole new lifestyle of
information.

Built to Last: Successful Habits of Visionary Companies

Ch. 7. Gerald R. Ford: The Collegial Executive—Ch. 8. Jimmy Carter: The Technocrat Executive—Ch. 9. Ronald Reagan: The Visionary Executive

Long Term Care insurance is a visionary product of the future that is here today.

I seduced myself into thinking I could enjoy both creative and fiscal success in the porn industry, getting drunk on the power of truly visionary pornography by the likes of Joey Silvera, John Leslie, Greg Dark, Elegant Angel-era Robert Black, etc.

Envisioneer is illiterate PRETENTIOUS LANGUAGE for *visionary*.

"Customers are encouraged to lean forward and interact with the site," said Craig Oliver, Web envisioneer of Club Intrawest.

Visualize and its variant forms, *revisualize, visualization*, and *revisualization*, have become popular extravagant substitutes for all manner of straightforward words, many of them associated with the imagination, which as a result is becoming exclusively ocular.

If you could visualize [imagine] the perfect place for growing potatoes, it would be Prince Edward Island.

The San Jacinto Museum of History, housed in the base of the monument, was chartered in 1938 to "preserve and revisualize [display] the history of early Texas."

The third characteristic of a reader is the ability to visualize [envision], revisualize [recall], or imagerize [imagine].

Please visualize [picture] what this means—it amounts to more than 40 classrooms of our children, an average size of 30 students each, murdered.

War Euphemisms. Much has changed since 1943 when Admiral William F. Halsey erected a billboard with the unambiguous message KILL JAPS, KILL JAPS, KILL MORE JAPS. Today politicians and military spokespeople find it better to be less explicit in matters of war. Acts and consequences are cloaked or turned topsy-turvy.

abuse, hazing, mistreatment, pranks = torture
administrator, ambassador = viceroy, proconsul
adviser = soldier, mercenary
aerial ordnance = bombs, missiles
area denial munitions, antipersonnel devices = land mines
attritting = killing
bomblet = bomb
caretaker government = occupying power, collaboration
    regime
civilian contractors, defense contractors = mercenaries, hired
    thugs
coercive persuasion, coercive techniques = torture
company doing business in Iraq = war profiteer
confinement facility, detention center = prison

conflict, counterproliferation, decisive force, incursion, interdiction, major combat operations, military action, military intervention, a military solution, pacification, the use of force = war, warfare

containment = blockade, siege

counterinsurgency, counterterrorism, covert action = terrorism, killing people

degrade = bomb

democratically minded strongman = dictator

destabilize the government = overthrow the government

directed energy weapon = death ray

disputed territories = occupied land

eliminate = kill

embedded journalist = censored reporter

enclosure = cell

enhanced interrogation tactics = torture

ethnic cleansing, social cleansing = slaughter, genocide, murder, forced deportation

exclusion zone = killing zone

hostilities = killing

impose sanctions = punish

improvised explosive device = homemade bomb

injured = wounded

liberation = invasion, occupation

liquidate = kill

Mark 77 firebombs = napalm

moderate physical pressure = torture

mop-up operation = shooting people

nation building = occupation, colonialism

neighborhood procedure = human shields

neutralize = kill, destroy, incapacitate
Operation Iraqi Freedom = invasion and occupation of Iraq
protectorate = colony
regional commander = warlord
relocation, transfer = forced deportation
remains = corpses, body parts
removal, wet work = assassination
reprisals = revenge
Rewards for Justice program = bounty
roll up = destroy, kill
security assistance force = occupying army
send a signal = threaten, intimidate [usually by bombing
    something or killing people]
sleep management = sleep deprivation
stabilization mission = occupation
a target-rich environment = easy pickings
ultimate justice, ultimate penalty, ultimate sanction = death
zone of conflict = battlefield

War on has been a metaphor to describe campaigns against illnesses and social evils since the turn of the twentieth century. Franklin Roosevelt's War on Polio and Lyndon Johnson's War on Poverty were fought with policy and legislation. But since Richard Nixon's War on Drugs and War on Crime, and especially since Ronald Reagan's War on Terrorism and George W. Bush's War on Terror, the metaphor has been forgotten and the battles have been fought with bombs and bullets. *War on* now justifies a military approach and all of the bloodshed and suspension of personal liberties that accompany it.

The War on Terrorism differs from the War on Terror. The former combats an activity, and thus is comparatively restricted. The latter combats an idea—an amorphous and elastic enemy—and thus can stretch on endlessly. What *terror* stands for is still unclear, but it may become a synonym for "all who frighten us"—in fact, it may be that already.

Weapons of mass destruction. It is only natural that a more dramatic phrase would be created to say *chemical and biological and possibly radioactive weapons.* Theatrical effect, however, sacrifices clarity. The United States, for example, used B-52 bombers, cruise missiles, tanks, cluster bombs, fuel-air bombs, and "bunker-buster" bombs in its invasion of Iraq, all of which massively destroyed life and property, yet few people in the U.S. saw them as weapons of mass destruction. Trucks, passenger jets, and fertilizer too have each proven to work as weapons of mass destruction, yet no one demanded an invasion of Iraq (or any other country) on the suspicion that it possessed trucks and passenger jets and fertilizer.

In his January 2004 State of the Union speech, President Bush further muddled things by announcing that the Iraq government had been guilty of *weapons of mass destruction–related program activities,* which alone justified its overthrow. This new doctrine means that almost any government on the planet now qualifies for PREEMPTION or REGIME change.

Weasel Words. When a dietary supplement company claims that its pill *supports healthy prostate function,* it is not a clumsy or pretentious way to say *heals your prostate* or even *helps your prostate*. It means exactly what it says: nothing. Weasel Words are carefully chosen to say something that sounds binding or verifiable, without actually saying anything of the sort.

advance, enhance, heighten, reform ≠ improve

affordable, bargain, economical, economically priced ≠ inexpensive

based on, inspired by ≠ adapted from [although even this term is weasely]

certified ≠ trustworthy or guaranteed

complimentary ≠ free

conclusively demonstrated ≠ proven

definitive, foremost, optimal ≠ best

educated, informed ≠ intelligent or wise

fair-minded, open ≠ fair

firmly committed to ≠ want to

is likely to, strives to, strive toward ≠ will

lawful, legal ≠ ethical [all behavior is lawful where no laws prohibit it]

limited ≠ brief

manageable ≠ safe

preferred ≠ good

reputable ≠ honest

resistant ≠ proof

timely ≠ prompt or quick

valued at ≠ worth

wellness ≠ health

winning strategy ≠ guarantee

See also VERBAL PRESTIDIGITATION.

Win, Win-win. As a noun, *win* has replaced *success*, as in *The arrival of wireless networks was a big win in 2002*. *Win-win*, a clichéd adjective, has replaced *successful*, as in *This is a win-win team*. *Win* comes from competitive sports, in which there can be only one winner, while *win-win* says that everybody wins. But *win-win*— as in *a win-win situation*—is most commonly a bogus sentiment, used by the winner to persuade the others that they are not losers, and by the losers to save face.

Zero-sum game. A zero-sum game, such as poker, is one in which one player's winnings are equal to the other players' losses. Human affairs, however, are not a game (at least not a well-ordered game). This GROOVY LINGO game theory term is a gross oversimplification when so used.

> Without freedom of press, a national convention or a constituent assembly will be a zero-sum game.

> The U.S. is obviously in a zero-sum game with terrorists.

> That is largely because any government allocation of resources—including racially preferential treatment—is a zero-sum game.

> The threads of her life just couldn't all be happy at the same time. She wondered if happiness was a zero-sum game. She decided to ignore the question and the unhappy threads and just acknowledge the happy threads today.

Zero tolerance is an emphatic way to say *intolerance* and narrows the range of permissible behavior. One cannot, of course, abide guns in schools or sexual predation in the office, but zero tolerance policies are also directed against much less heinous offenses such as profanity, disobedience, loitering, and the like— whose criminality is wholly subjective.

Curiously, one never hears of a zero tolerance policy for, say, executive fraud or lying by politicians.

Following complaints by business owners, residents, and visitors, the Brockport Police Department will be operating on zero tolerance level on loitering on Main Street and other sections of the village.

Among disciplinary actions mandated by zero tolerance policies, suspension is most frequently used for an extensive range of common offenses, from attendance problems to disrespect and noncompliance.

Michigan State University has established a Zero Tolerance Policy, which is in effect 24 hours per day, seven days per week, against noise.

Dalrymple calls for "zero tolerance" on the matter. Baseball caps must be banned.

In Texas, a zero tolerance dress code has led to over 800 suspensions since the school year began, most for students wearing their shirts untucked.

A police officer who was suspended after he refused to arrest a homeless man for trespassing said his superiors told his unit, "Zero tolerance, we will not make deals with the homeless."